RECORDED ACCOMPANIMENTS ONLINE

MEN'S EDITION

ANDREW LLOYD WEBBER™

THEATRE SONGS

To access companion recorded accompaniments online, visit:
www.halleonard.com/mylibrary

Enter Code
2426-3641-3115-9619

Andrew Lloyd Webber™ is a trademark owned by Andrew Lloyd Webber.

ISBN 978-1-5400-2439-8

HAL•LEONARD®

Visit Hal Leonard Online at
www.halleonard.com

Contact Us:
Hal Leonard
7777 West Bluemound Road
Milwaukee, WI 53213
Email: info@halleonard.com

In Europe contact:
Hal Leonard Europe Limited
Distribution Centre, Newmarket Road
Bury St Edmunds, Suffolk, IP33 3YB
Email: info@halleonardeurope.com

In Australia contact:
Hal Leonard Australia Pty. Ltd.
4 Lentara Court
Cheltenham, Victoria, 3192 Australia
Email: info@halleonard.com.au

CONTENTS

Pianists on the Full Version Recordings:
[1] Brian Dean   [2] Brendan Fox   [3] Richard Walters

Pianists on the 16-Bar Recordings:
* Brendan Fox   ** Richard Walters

ANY DREAM WILL DO
from *Joseph and the Amazing Technicolor® Dreamcoat*

Music by ANDREW LLOYD WEBBER
Lyrics by TIM RICE

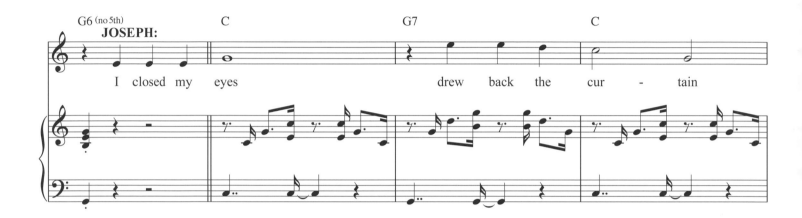

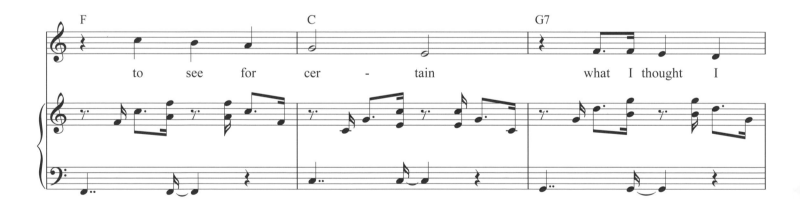

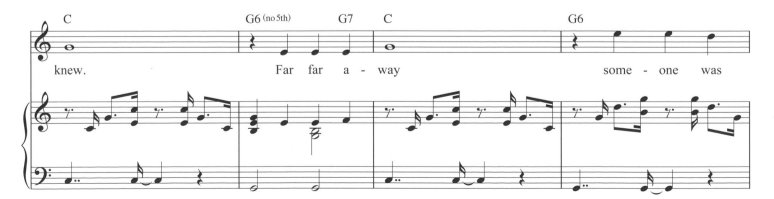

weep - ing, but the world was sleep - ing,

an - y dream will do. I wore my coat

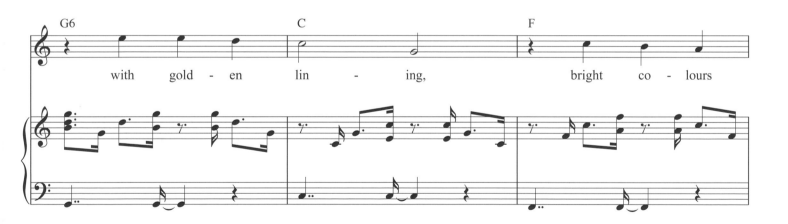

with gold - en lin - ing, bright co - lours

shin - ing won - der - ful and new.

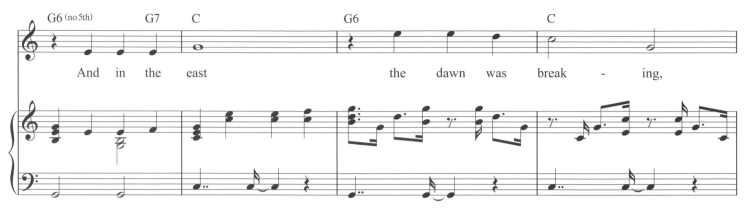

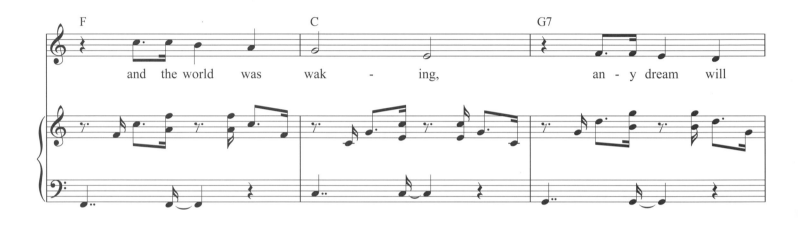

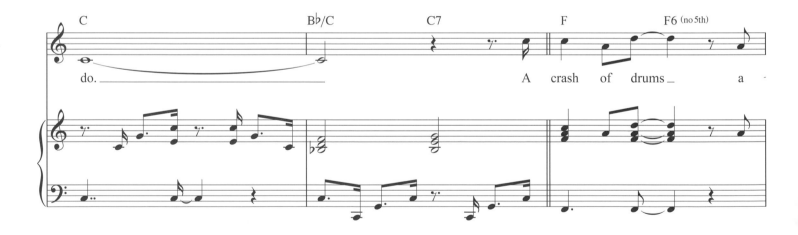

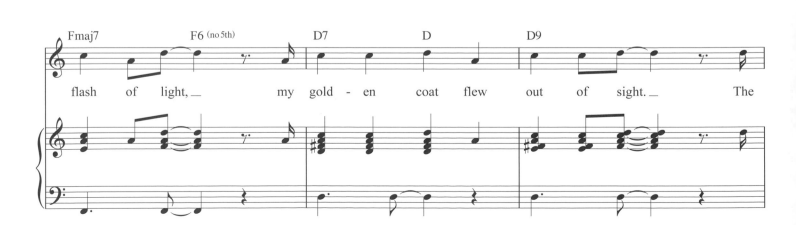

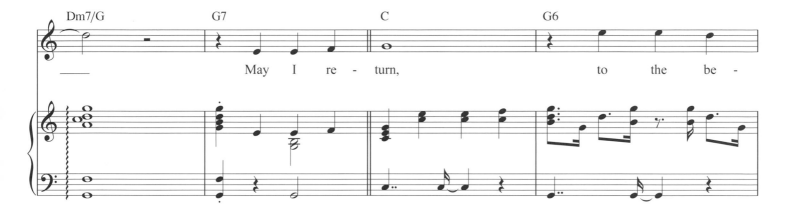

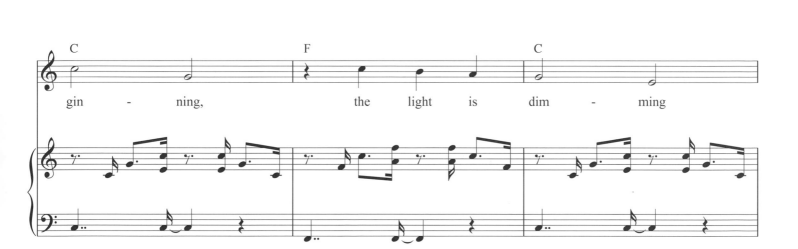

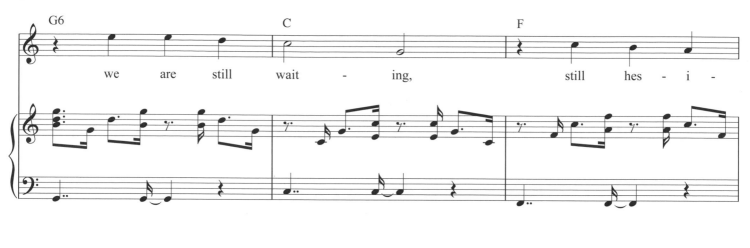

we are still wait - ing, still hes - i -

ta - ting an - y dream will do,

an - y dream will do,

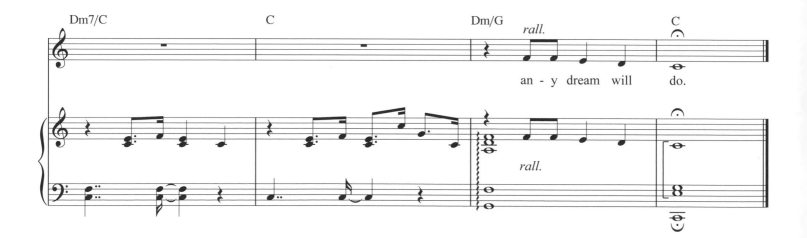

an - y dream will do.

ANY DREAM WILL DO

from *Joseph and the Amazing Technicolor® Dreamcoat*

excerpt

Music by ANDREW LLOYD WEBBER
Lyrics by TIM RICE

THE BALLAD OF BILLY M'CAW
from *Cats*

Music by ANDREW LLOYD WEBBER
Text by T.S. ELIOT

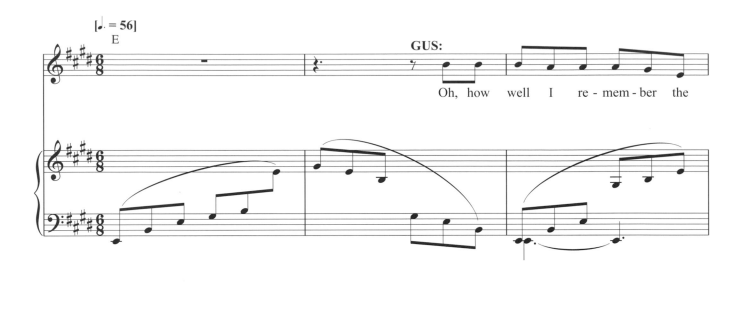

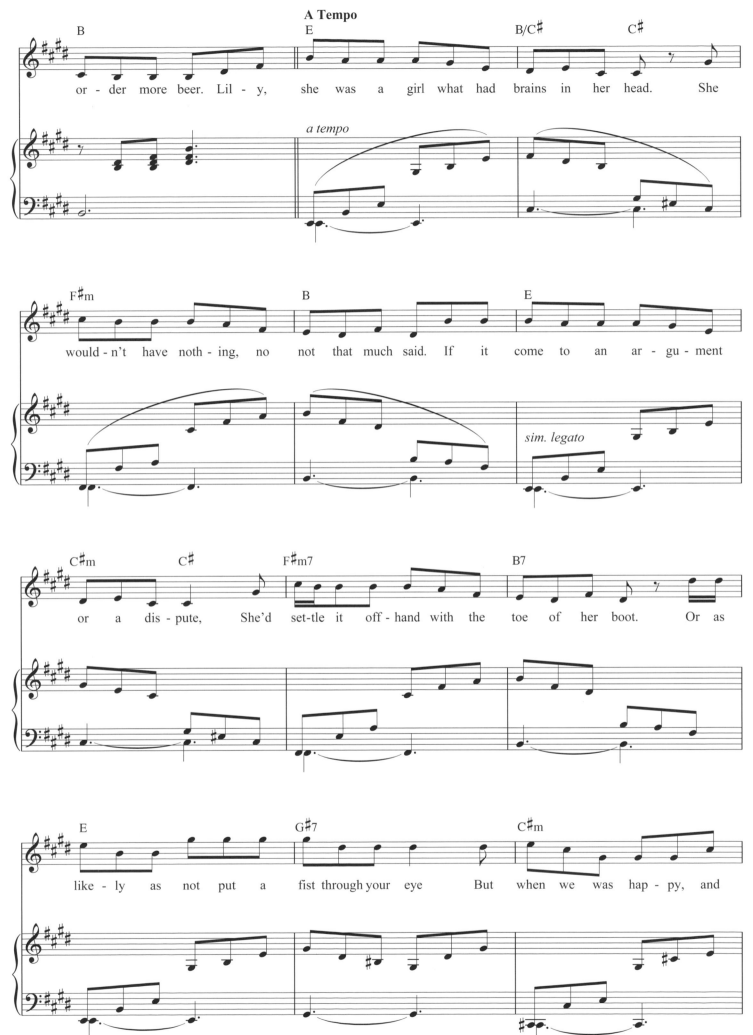

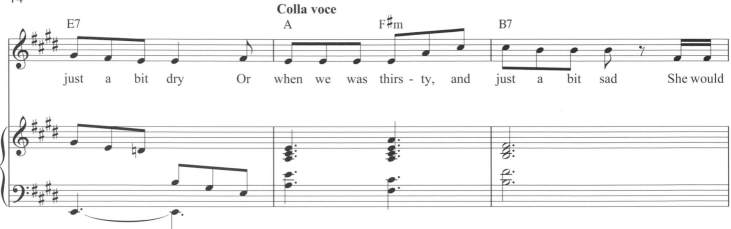

just a bit dry Or when we was thirs-ty, and just a bit sad She would

rap on the bar with that cork-screw she had And sing "Bil - ly, Bil - ly M'-
"Bil - ly, Bil - ly M'-

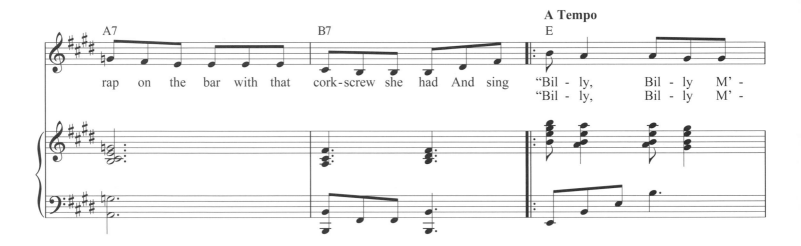

Caw! _____ Come give us a tune on your pas-to-ral flute!" And
Caw! _____ Come give us a tune on your mo-ley gui-tar!" And

Bil - ly'd strike up on his pas-to-ral flute. And Bil - ly'd strike up on his
Bil - ly'd strike up on his mo-ley gui-tar. And Bil - ly'd strike up on his

THE BALLAD OF BILLY M'CAW
from *Cats*
excerpt

Music by ANDREW LLOYD WEBBER
Text by T.S. ELIOT

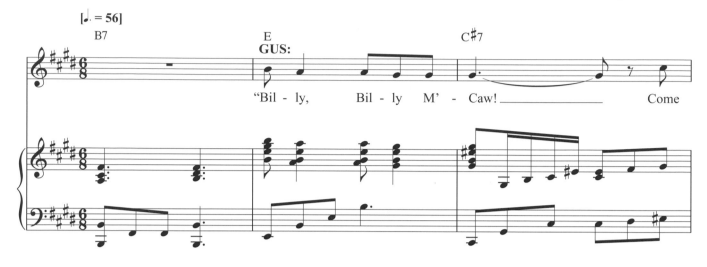

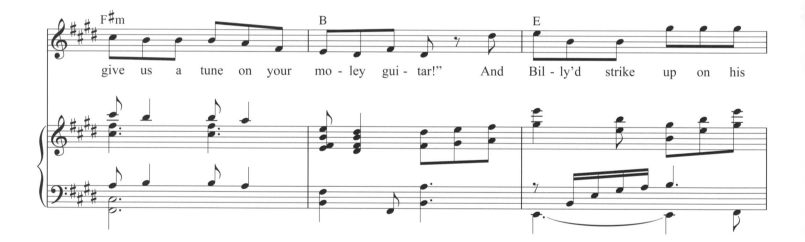

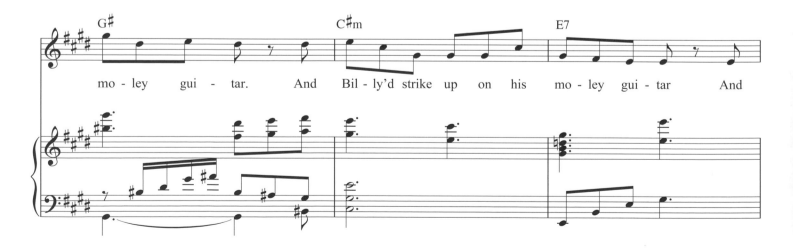

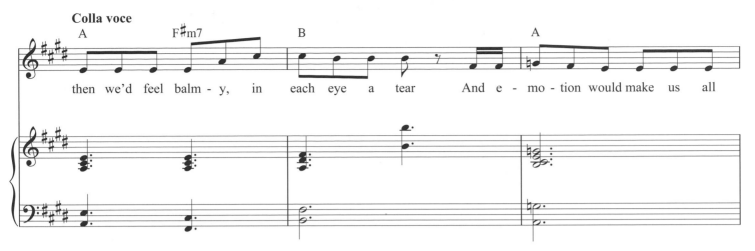

then we'd feel balm-y, in each eye a tear And e - mo - tion would make us all

or - der more beer. Bil - ly! Bil - ly M' - Caw! _____ Come

give us a tune on your mo - ley gui - tar! Ah! He was the life of the bar.

CLOSE EVERY DOOR

from *Joseph and the Amazing Technicolor® Dreamcoat*

Music by ANDREW LLOYD WEBBER
Lyrics by TIM RICE

Espressivo

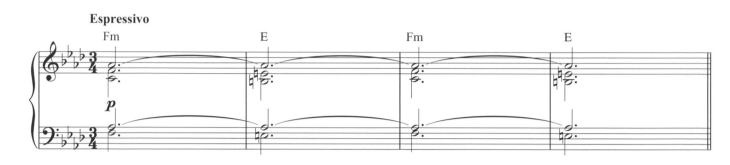

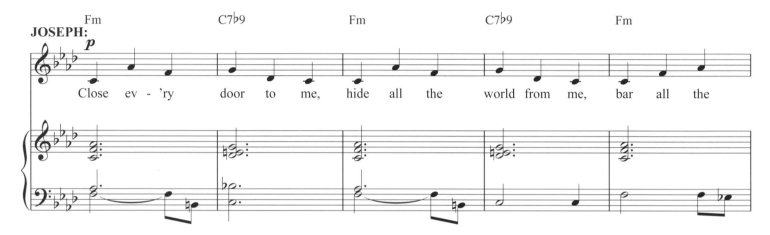

JOSEPH:
Close ev-'ry door to me, hide all the world from me, bar all the

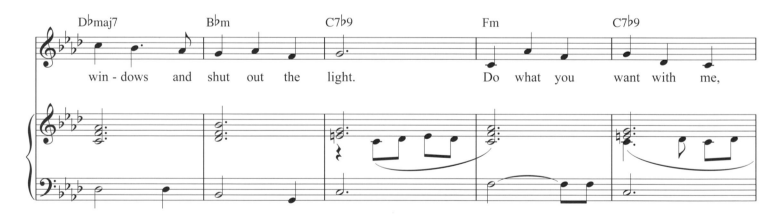

win-dows and shut out the light. Do what you want with me,

hate me and laugh at me, dark-en my day-time and tor-ture my

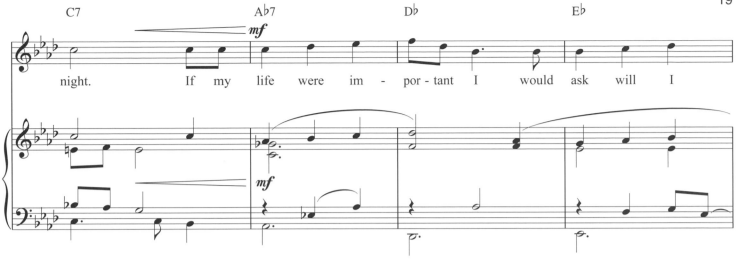

night. If my life were im-por-tant I would ask will I

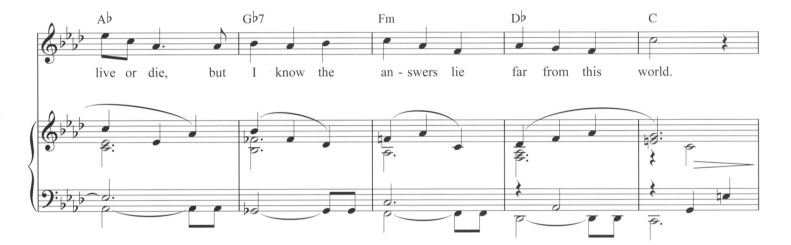

live or die, but I know the an-swers lie far from this world.

Close ev-'ry door to me, keep those I love from me,

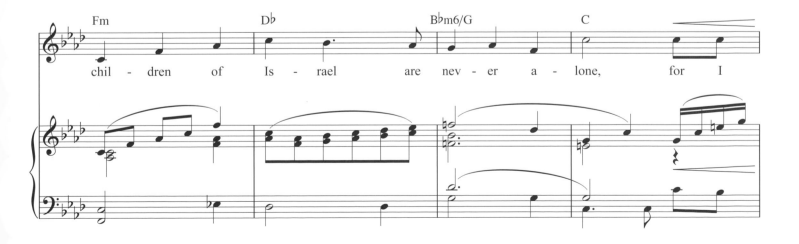

chil-dren of Is-rael are nev-er a-lone, for I

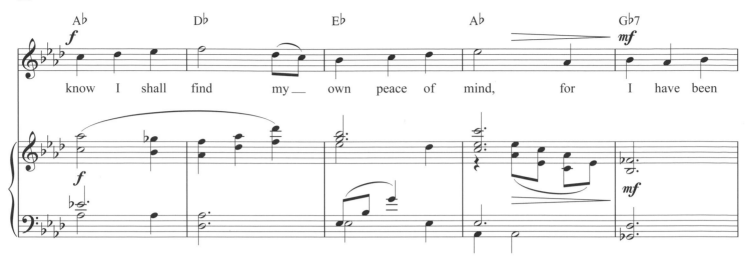

know I shall find my___ own peace of mind, for I have been

prom - ised a land__ of my own.

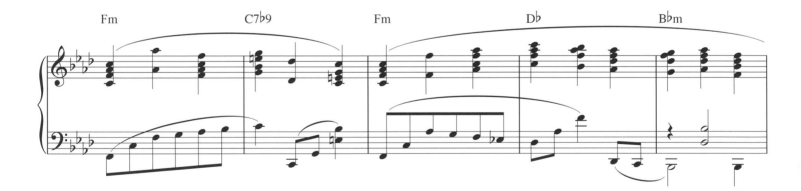

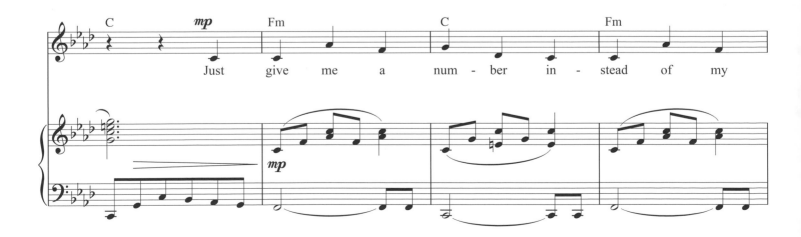

Just give me a num - ber in - stead of my

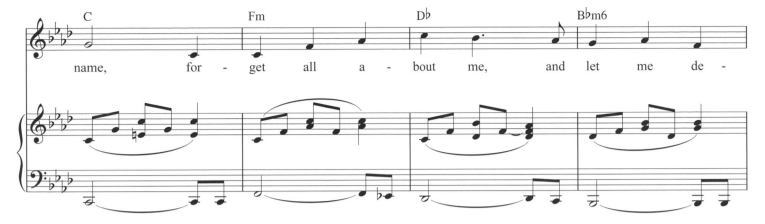

name, for - get all a - bout me, and let me de -

cay. I do not mat - ter, I'm on - ly one per - son, de -

stroy me com - plete - ly, then throw me a - way. If my life were im -

por - tant I would ask will I live or die, but I know the an - swers lie

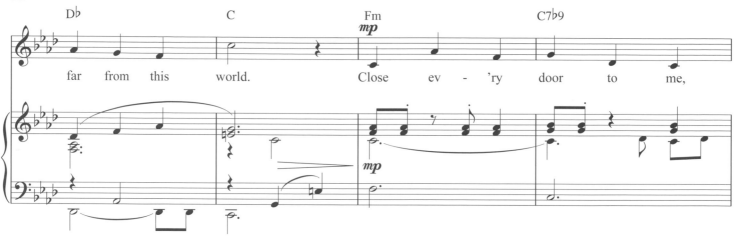

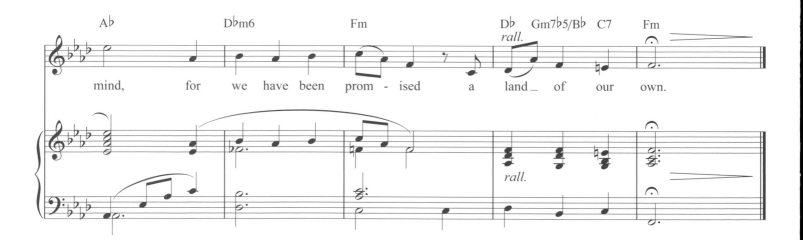

CLOSE EVERY DOOR

from *Joseph and the Amazing Technicolor® Dreamcoat*

excerpt

Music by ANDREW LLOYD WEBBER
Lyrics by TIM RICE

EVERMORE WITHOUT YOU
from *The Woman in White*

Music by ANDREW LLOYD WEBBER
Lyrics by DAVID ZIPPEL

Semplice

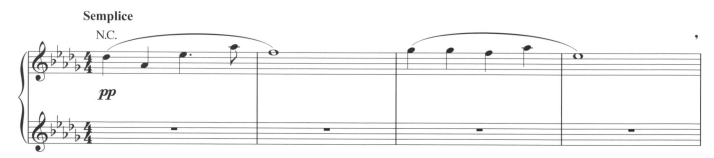

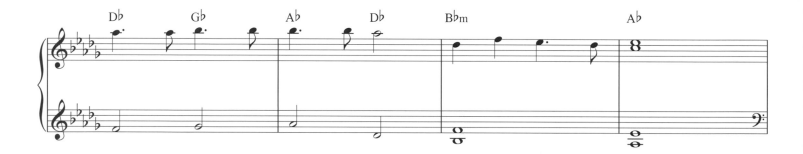

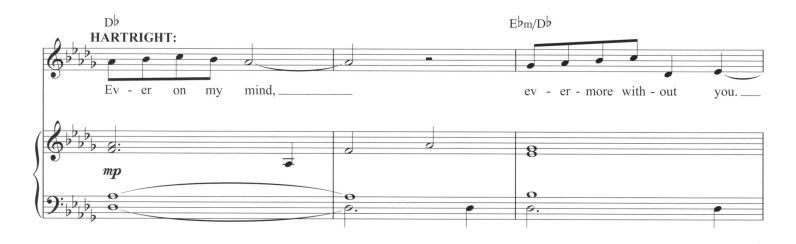

HARTRIGHT:

Ev - er on my mind, _____ ev - er - more with - out you. _____

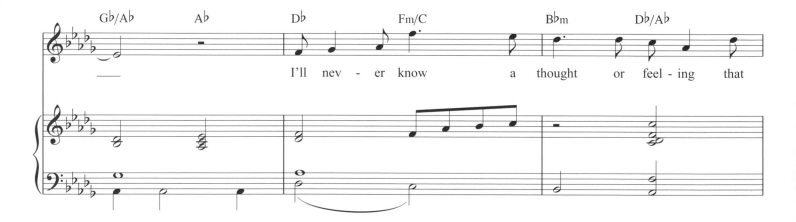

_____ I'll nev - er know a thought or feel - ing that

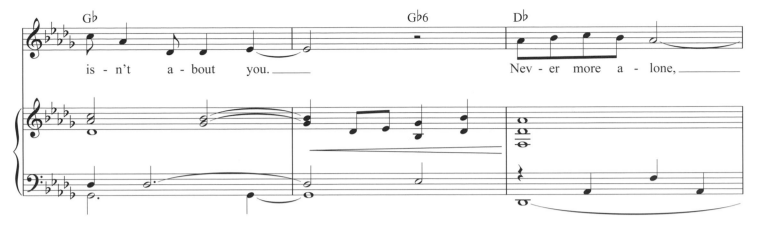

is - n't a - bout you. _____ Nev - er more a - lone, _____

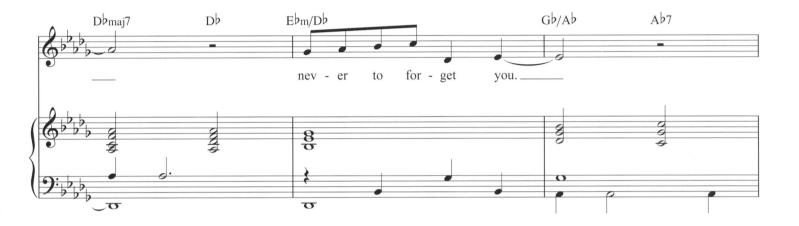

_____ nev - er to for - get you. _____

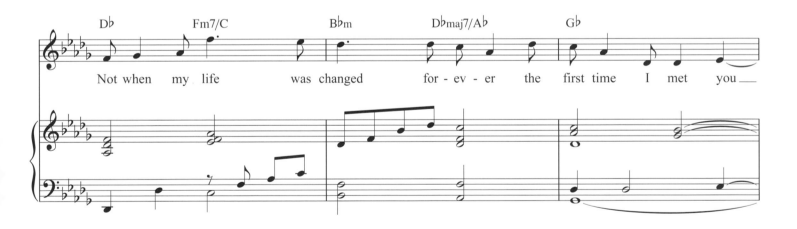

Not when my life was changed for - ev - er the first time I met you _____

_____ You're all I know and though I've lost you, you're

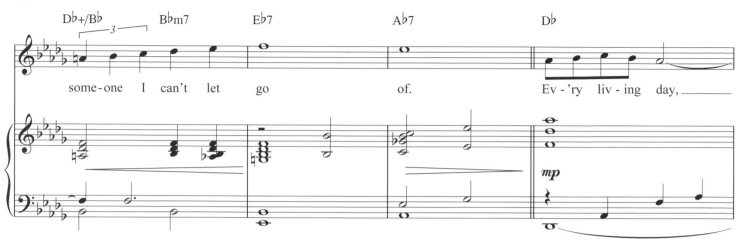

some-one I can't let go of. Ev -'ry liv - ing day, ___

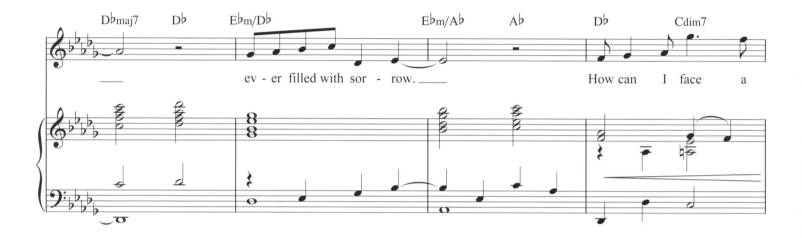

___ ev - er filled with sor - row. ___ How can I face a

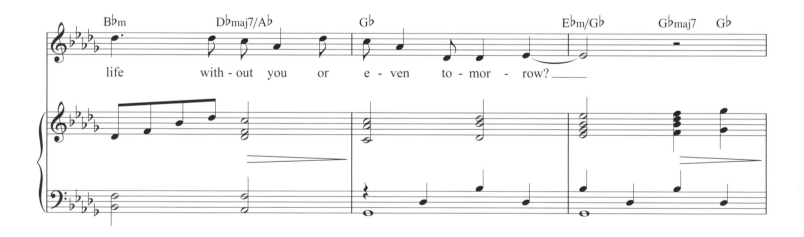

life with - out you or e - ven to - mor - row? ___

Ev - er - more with - out you, ___ Were we nev - er meant to

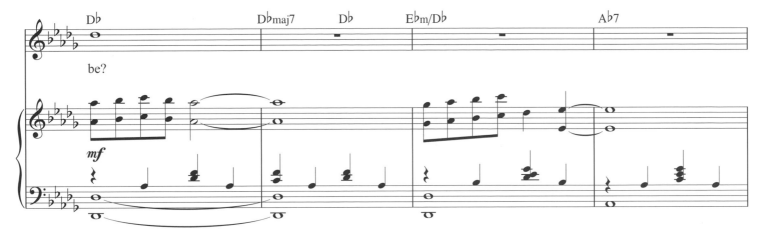

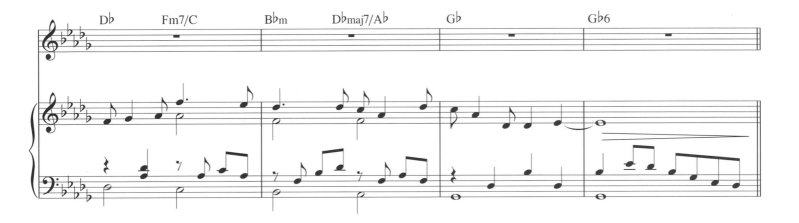

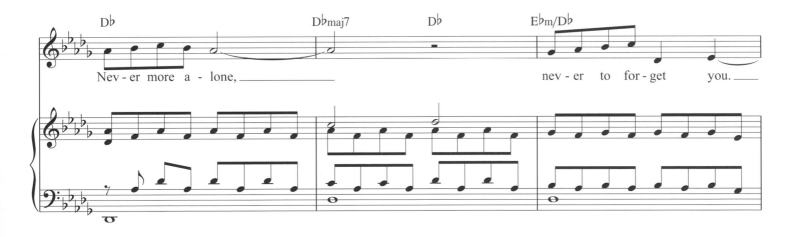

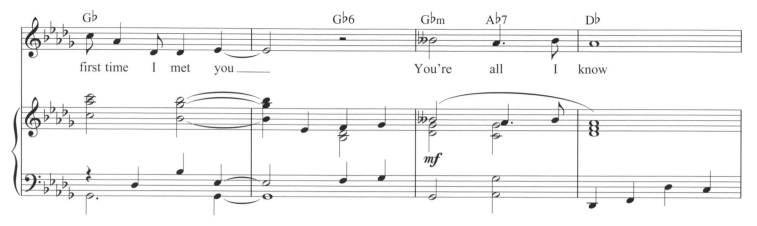

first time I met you _____ You're all I know

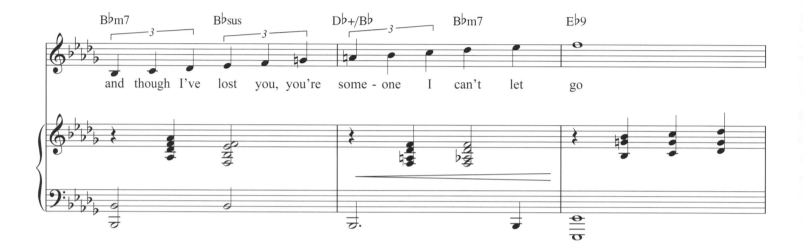

and though I've lost you, you're some - one I can't let go

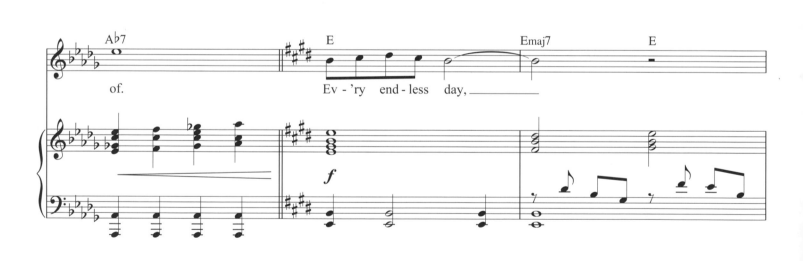

of. Ev - 'ry end - less day, _____

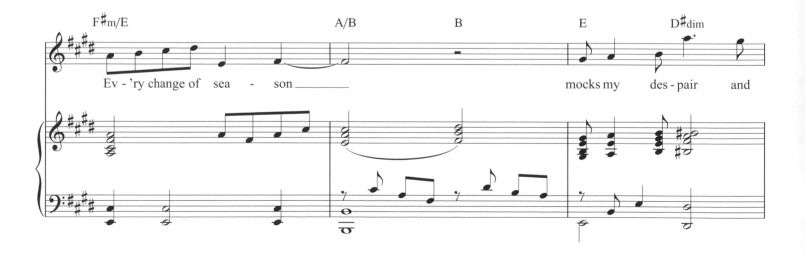

Ev - 'ry change of sea - son _____ mocks my des - pair and

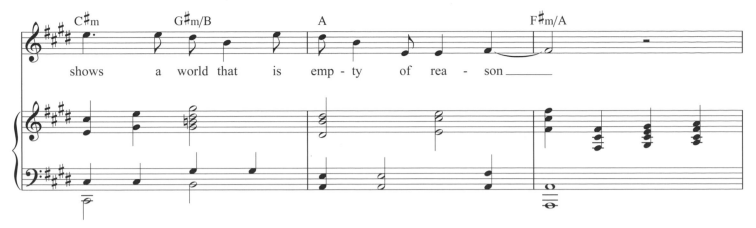

shows a world that is emp-ty of rea - son

Ev - er - more with-out you. _____ Were we nev - er meant to

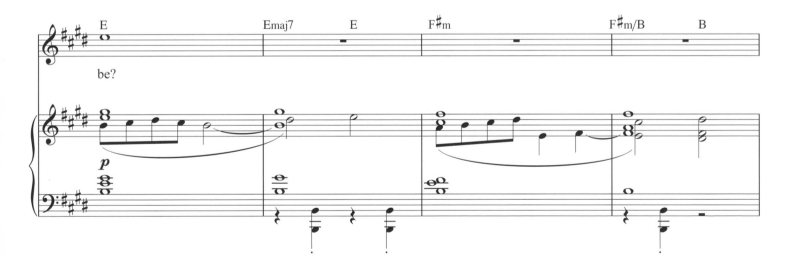

be?

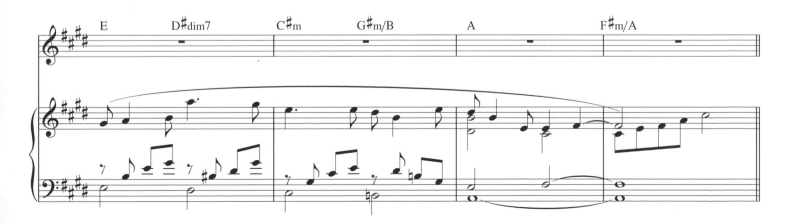

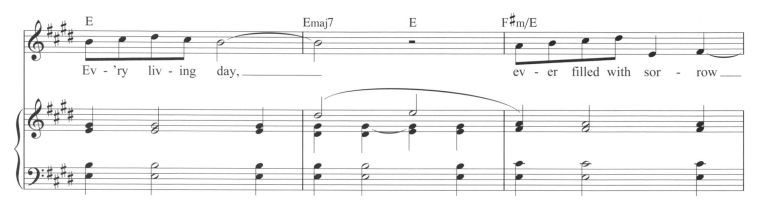

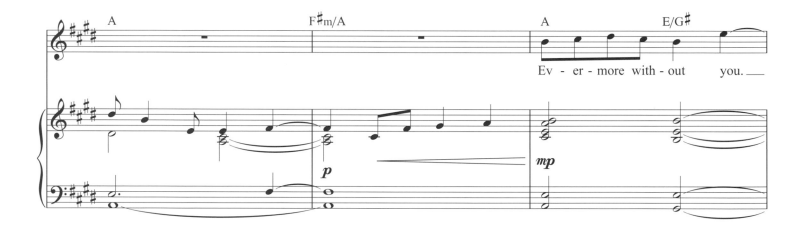

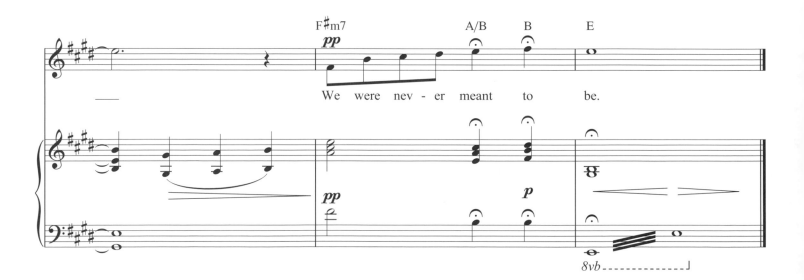

EVERMORE WITHOUT YOU

from *The Woman in White*

excerpt

Music by ANDREW LLOYD WEBBER
Lyrics by DAVID ZIPPEL

HEAVEN ON THEIR MINDS

from *Jesus Christ Superstar*

Words by TIM RICE
Music by ANDREW LLOYD WEBBER

Moderate Rock tempo

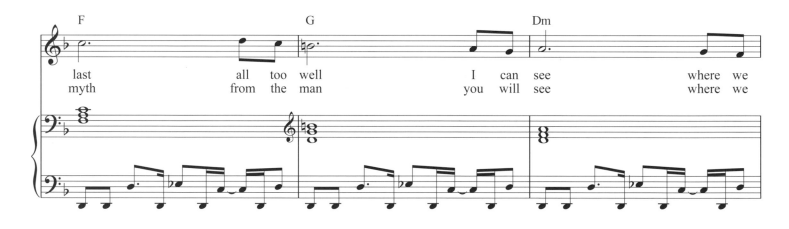

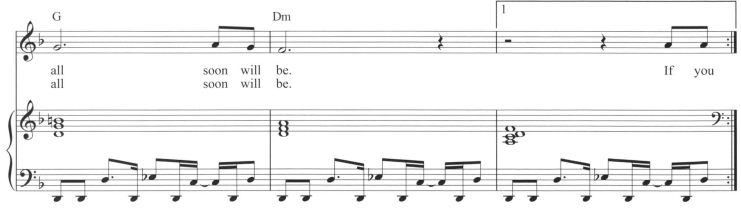

Je - sus! _____ You've

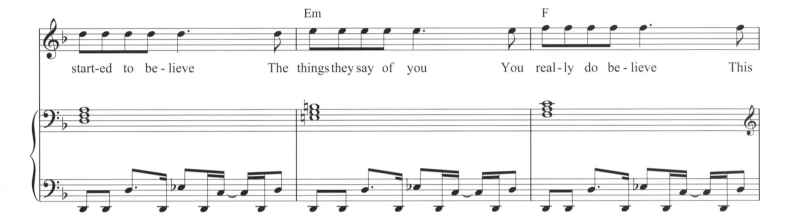

start-ed to be-lieve The things they say of you You real-ly do be-lieve This

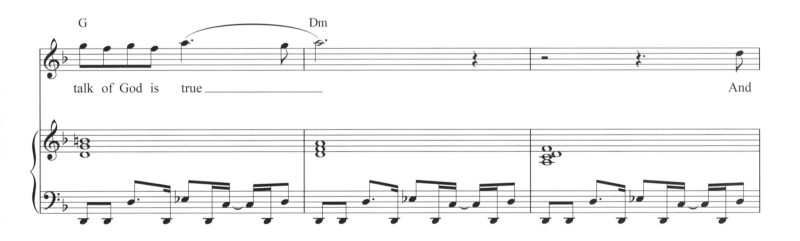

talk of God is true _____ And

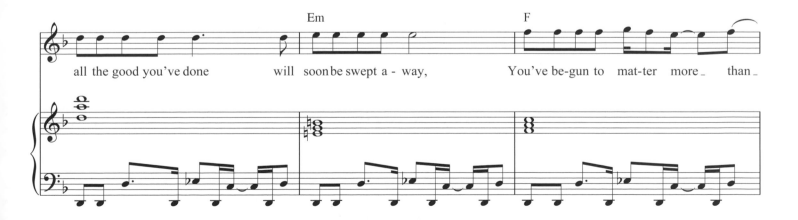

all the good you've done will soon be swept a - way, You've be-gun to mat-ter more _ than _

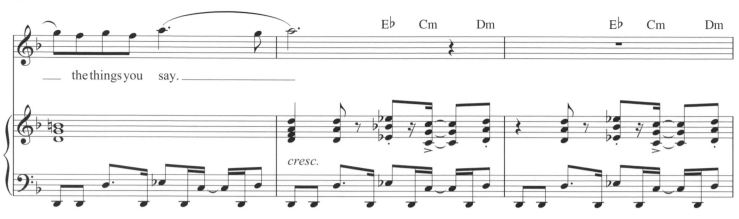

the things you say.

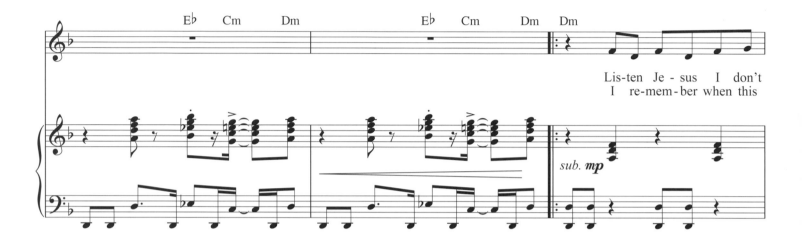

Lis-ten Je - sus I don't
I re-mem - ber when this

like what I see ___ All I ask is that you lis - ten to me
whole thing be - gan ___ No talk of God then we called you a man

And re - mem - ber— I've been your right hand man ___ all a - long.
And be - lieve me— my ad - mi - ra - tion for you has - n't died ___

You have set them all on fire
But ev-'ry word you say to-day

They think they've
Gets twist-ed

found the new Mes-si-ah
'round some oth-er way

And they'll hurt you when they find they're
And they'll hurt you if they think you've

wrong.

lied.

Naz-a-reth your fa-mous son should have stayed a great un-known

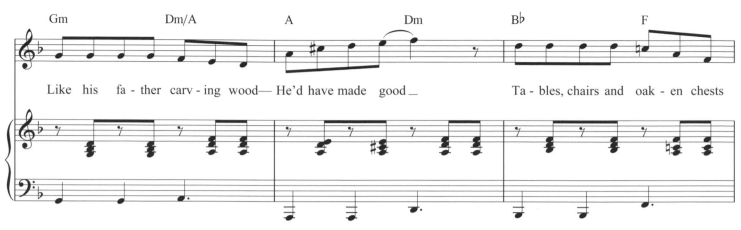

Like his fa - ther carv - ing wood— He'd have made good _ Ta - bles, chairs and oak - en chests

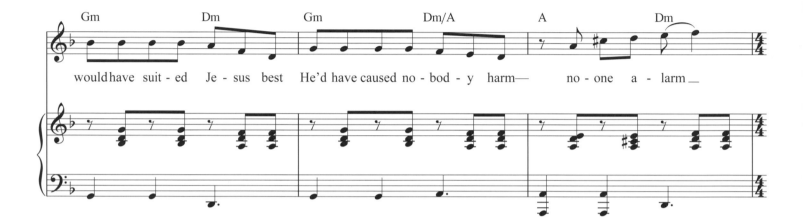

would have suit - ed Je - sus best He'd have caused no - bod - y harm— no - one a - larm _

Lis - ten Je - sus do you care for your race? _____
Lis - ten Je - sus to the warn - ing I give _____

Don't you see we must keep in our place?
Please re - mem - ber that I want us to live

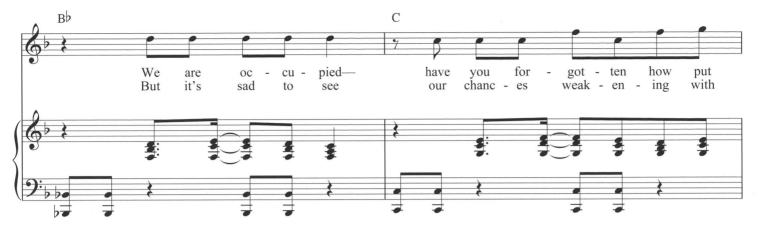

We are oc - cu - pied—
But it's sad to see

have you for - got - ten how put
our chanc - es weak - en - ing with

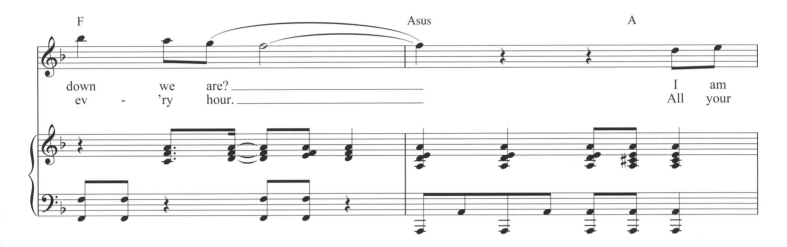

down we are?_____
ev - 'ry hour._____

I am
All your

fright - ened by the crowd
fol - low - ers are blind

For we are
Too much

get - ting much too loud __
heav - en on their minds __

And they'll crush us if we go too
It was beau - ti - ful but now it's

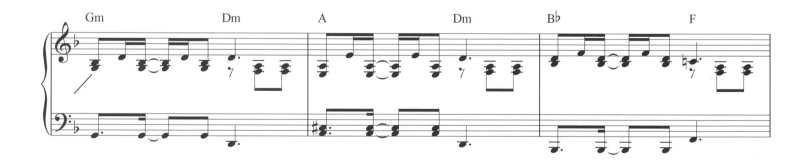

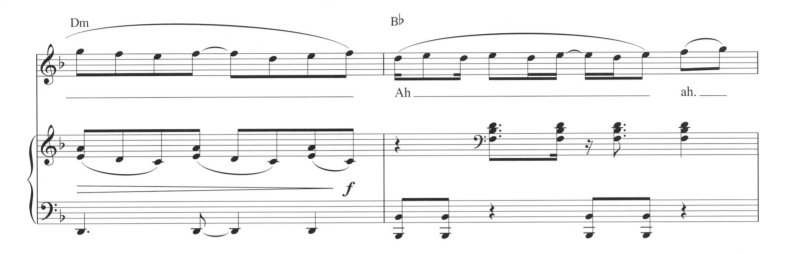

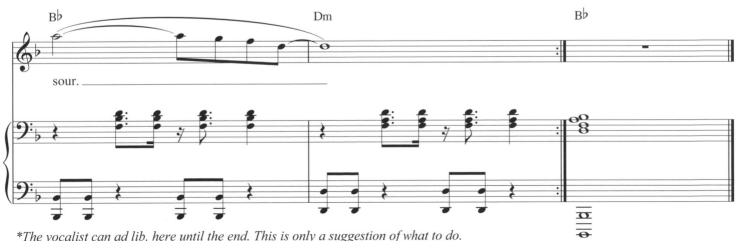

The vocalist can ad lib. here until the end. This is only a suggestion of what to do.

HEAVEN ON THEIR MINDS

from *Jesus Christ Superstar*

excerpt

Words by TIM RICE
Music by ANDREW LLOYD WEBBER

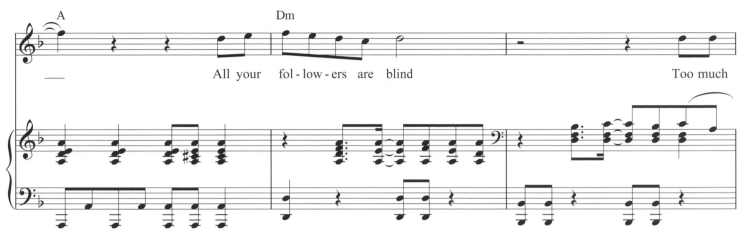

All your fol-low-ers are blind   Too much

heav-en on their minds ___   It was beau-ti-ful but now it's

sour, ___   Yes it's all ___ gone ___

sour. ___

I ONLY WANT TO SAY
(Gethsemane)
from *Jesus Christ Superstar*

Words by TIM RICE
Music by ANDREW LLOYD WEBBER

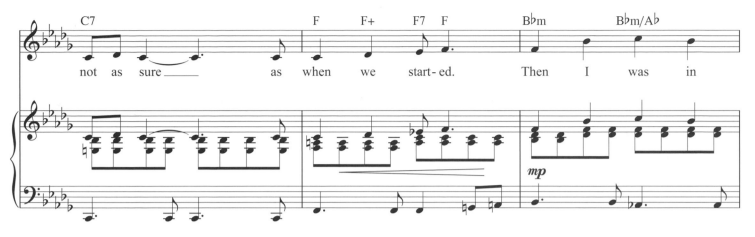

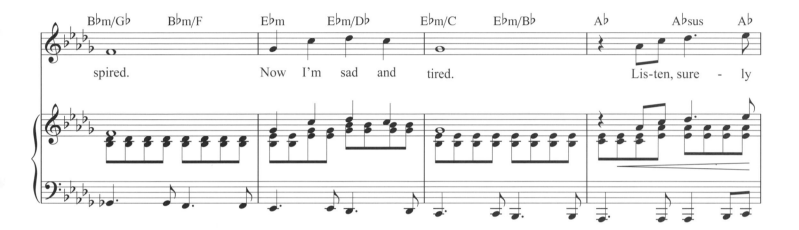

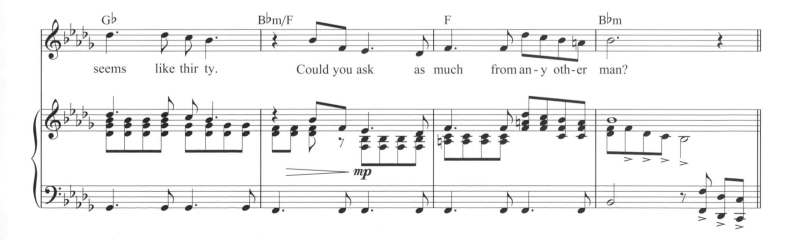

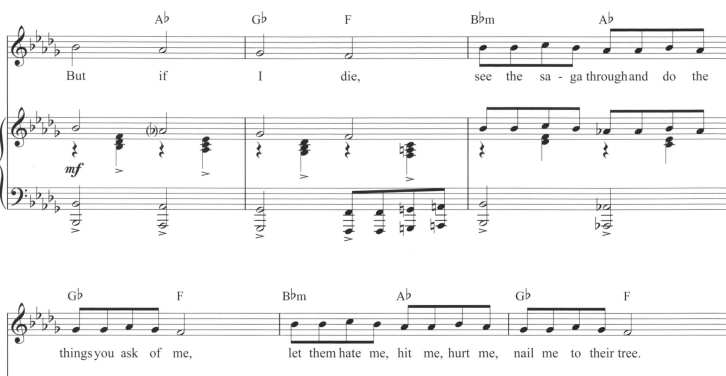

But if I die, see the sa - ga through and do the

things you ask of me, let them hate me, hit me, hurt me, nail me to their tree.

I'd wan - na know, I'd wan - na know my God. I'd wan - na know, I'd wan - na know my God.

I'd wan - na see, I'd wan - na see my God. I'd wan - na see, I'd wan - na see my God.

If I die what will __ be my re - ward? If I die what will __ be my re - ward?

I'd have to know, I'd have __ to know my Lord. __ I'd have to know, I'd have __ to know my Lord. __

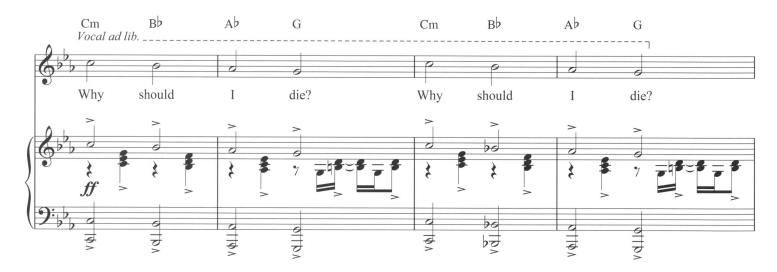

Vocal ad lib.

Why should I die? Why should I die?

Can you show me now that I would not be killed in vain? Show me just a lit - tle of your

om - ni - pres - ent brain. Show me there's a rea-son for your want-ing me to die. You're

far too keen on where and how and not so hot on why. Al - right

I'll die! Just watch me die!

See how I die! See how

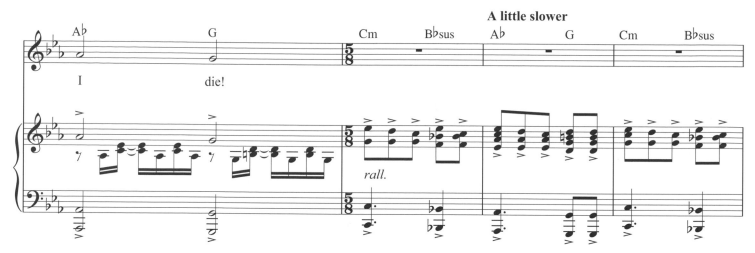

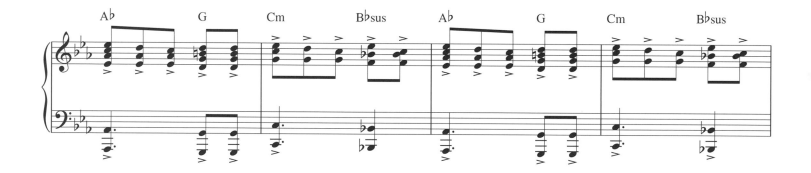

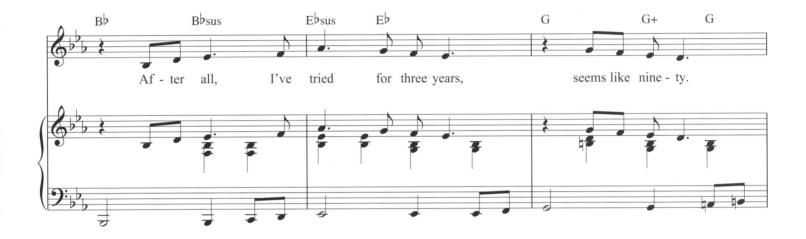

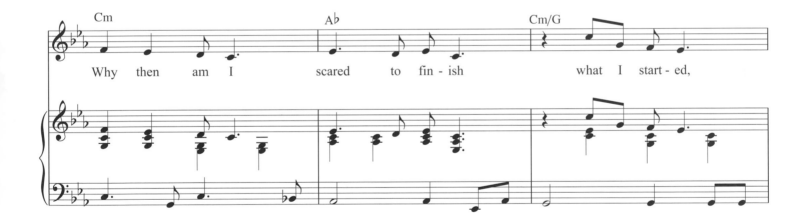

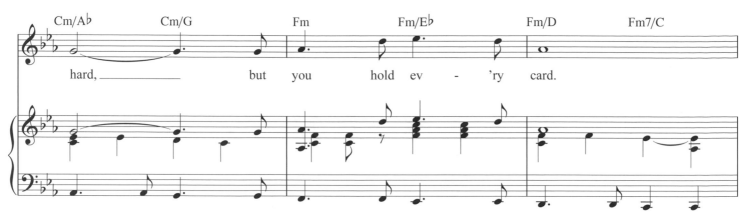

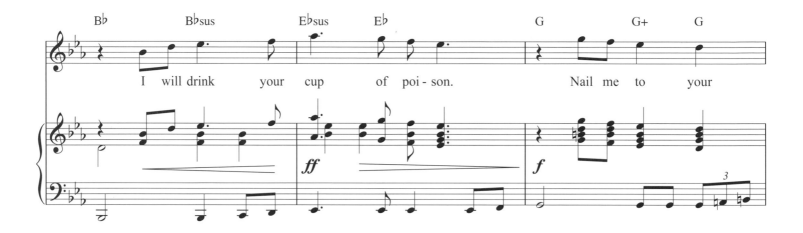

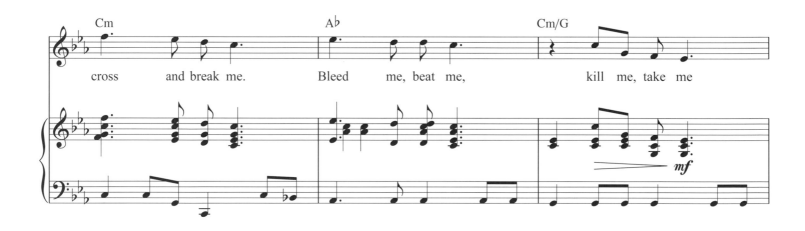

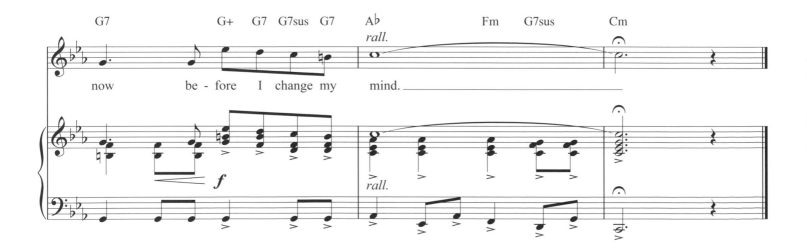

I ONLY WANT TO SAY

(Gethsemane)

from *Jesus Christ Superstar*

excerpt

Words by TIM RICE
Music by ANDREW LLOYD WEBBER

KING HEROD'S SONG

from *Jesus Christ Superstar*

Music by ANDREW LLOYD WEBBER
Lyrics by TIM RICE

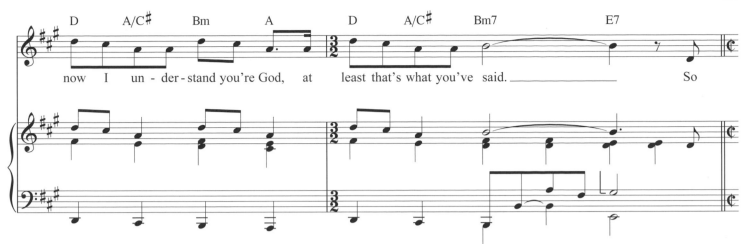

now I un - der - stand you're God, at least that's what you've said. _____ So

Moderato, Ragtime style

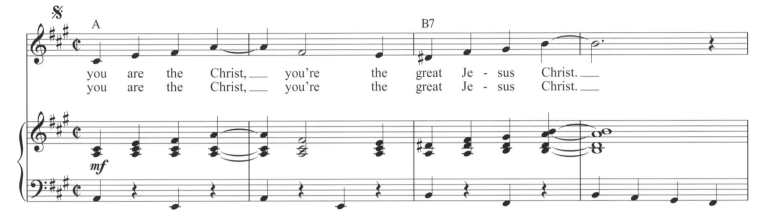

you are the Christ, ___ you're the great Je - sus Christ. ___
you are the Christ, ___ you're the great Je - sus Christ. ___

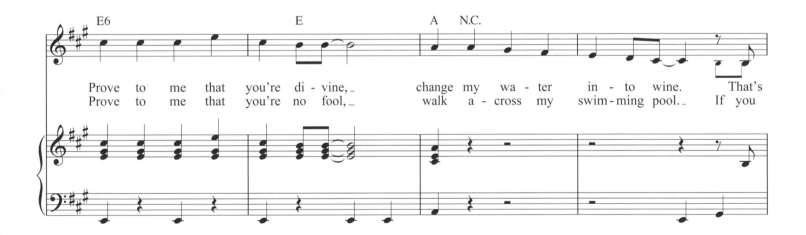

Prove to me that you're di - vine, _ change my wa - ter in - to wine. That's
Prove to me that you're no fool, _ walk a - cross my swim - ming pool. _ If you

all you need do _____ and I'll know it's all true, _____
do that for me _____ then I'll let you go free, _____

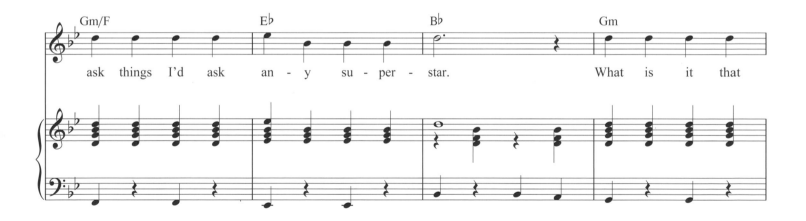
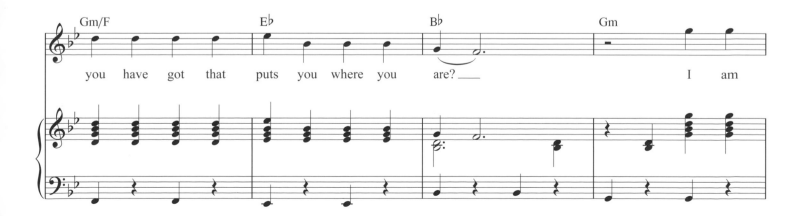
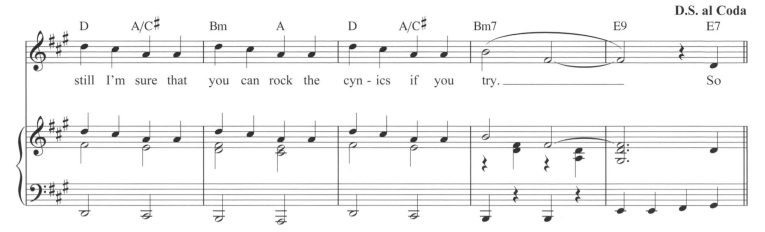

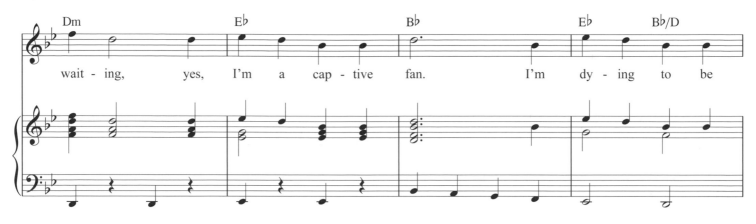

wait - ing, yes, I'm a cap - tive fan. I'm dy - ing to be

shown that you are not just an - y man. _____ So if

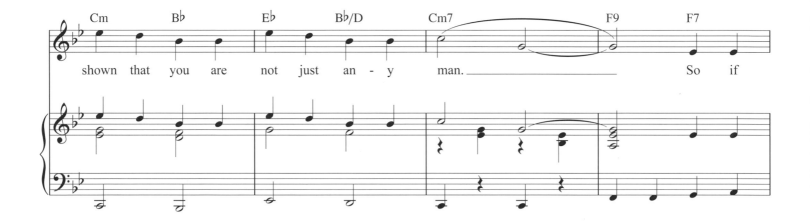

you are the Christ, ___ yes, the great Je - sus Christ, ___

feed my house - hold with this bread, _ you can do it on your head. Or has

some - thing gone wrong? __ Why do you take so long? __

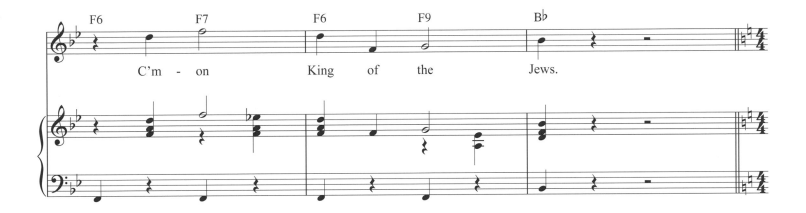

C'm - on King of the Jews.

Slowly, dramatically

Hey! Aren't you scared of me, Christ? _ Mis - ter Won - der - ful Christ! _

You're a joke, you're not the Lord, _ you're noth - ing but a fraud. _

Moderato, Ragtime style

This page has been left blank to facilitate page turns.

KING HEROD'S SONG
from *Jesus Christ Superstar*
excerpt

Music by ANDREW LLOYD WEBBER
Lyrics by TIM RICE

Moderato, Ragtime Style

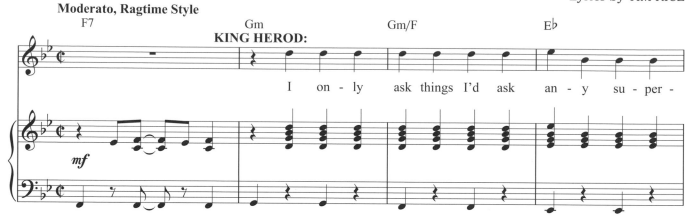

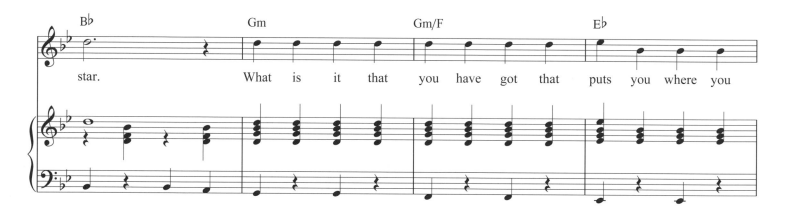

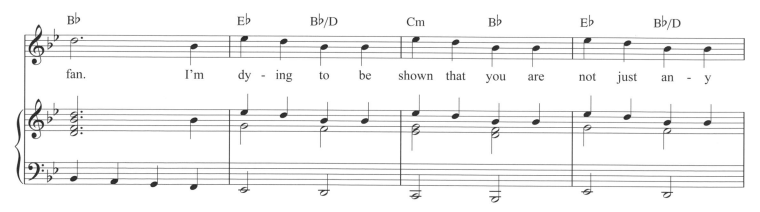

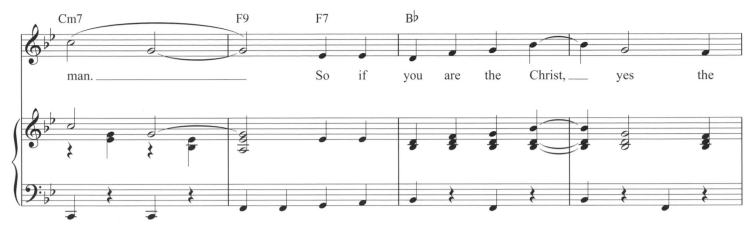

man. _____ So if you are the Christ, ___ yes the

great Je - sus Christ, ___ Feed my house - hold with this bread; ___

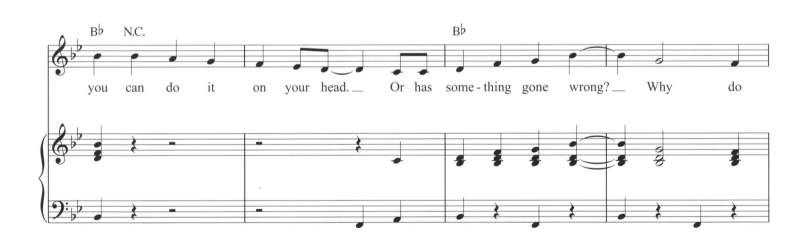

you can do it on your head. ___ Or has some - thing gone wrong? ___ Why do

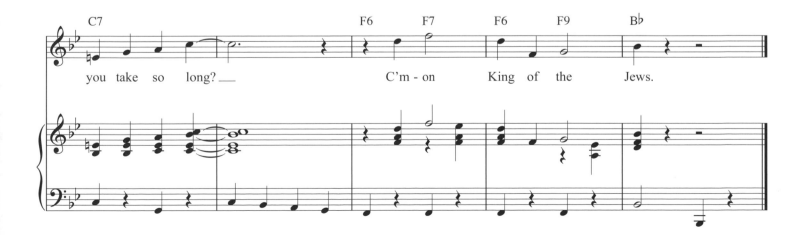

you take so long? ___ C'm - on King of the Jews.

LOVE CHANGES EVERYTHING
from *Aspects of Love*

Music by ANDREW LLOYD WEBBER
Lyrics by DON BLACK and CHARLES HART

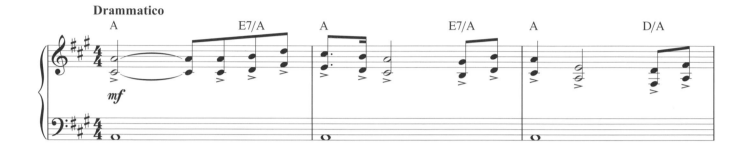

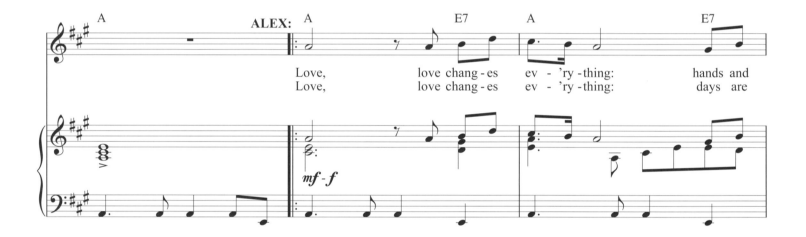

ev - 'ry - thing: how you live and how you die.
strong - est heart, pain is deep - er than be - fore.

Love _____ can make the sum - mer fly or a night seem like a
Love _____ will turn your world a - round and that world will last for -

life - time. Yes love, _____ love chang - es ev - 'ry - thing: now I
ev - er. Yes love, _____ love chang - es ev - 'ry - thing; brings you

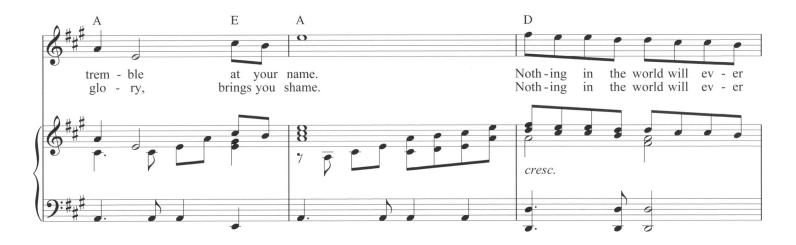

trem - ble at your name. Noth - ing in the world will ev - er
glo - ry, brings you shame. Noth - ing in the world will ev - er

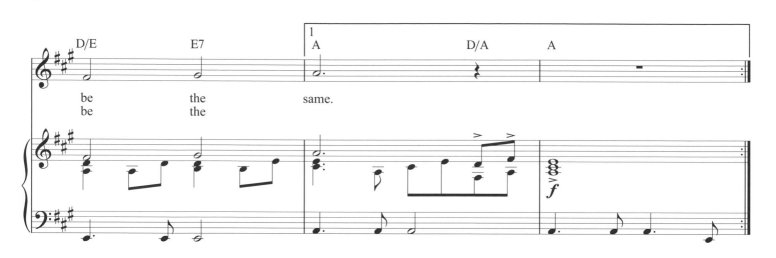

be   the   same.

be   the

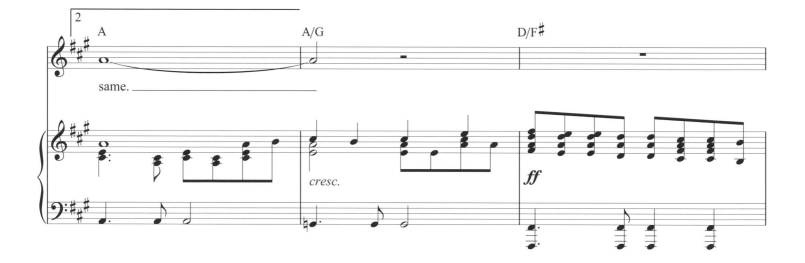

same. _____

Off _____ in - to the world we go,   plan - ning fu - tures,   shap - ing

years. Love _____ bursts in and sud-den-ly, all our

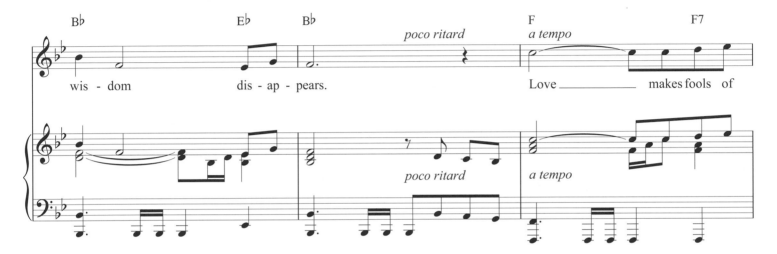

wis - dom dis-ap-pears. Love _____ makes fools of

ev - ery-one: all the rules we make are bro - ken. Yes

love, _____ love chang-es ev - 'ry-thing. Live or per - ish in its

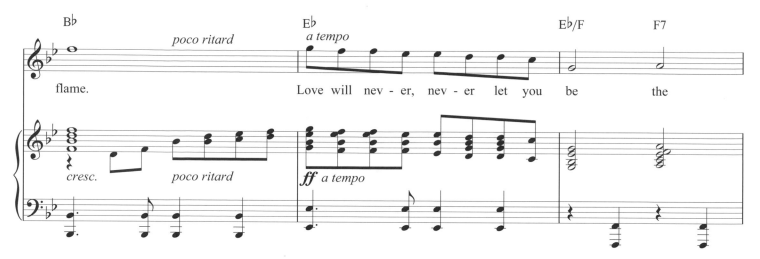

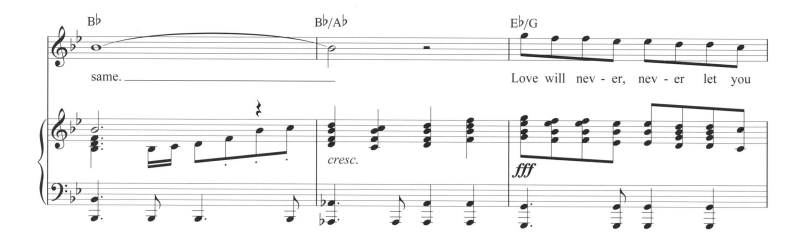

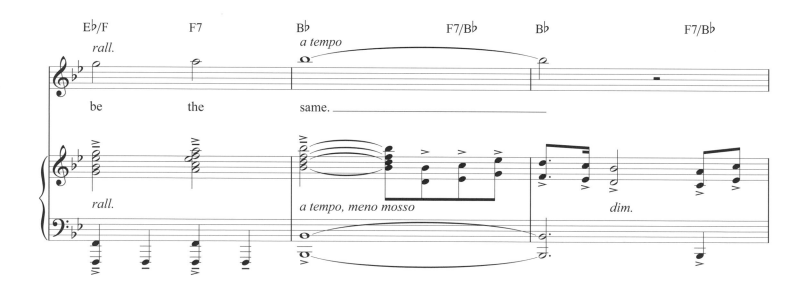

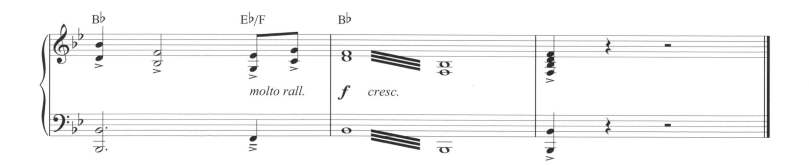

LOVE CHANGES EVERYTHING

from *Aspects of Love*

excerpt

Music by ANDREW LLOYD WEBBER
Lyrics by DON BLACK and CHARLES HART

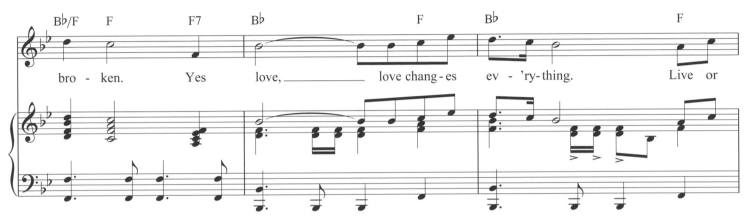

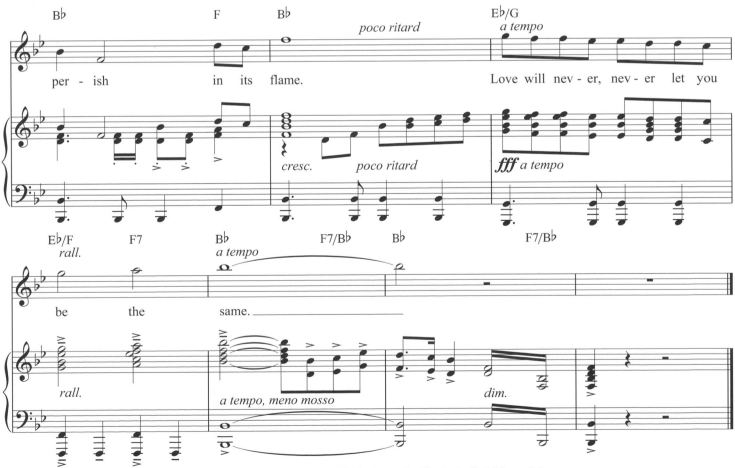

MEMORY
from *Cats*

Music by ANDREW LLOYD WEBBER
Text by TREVOR NUNN after T.S. ELIOT

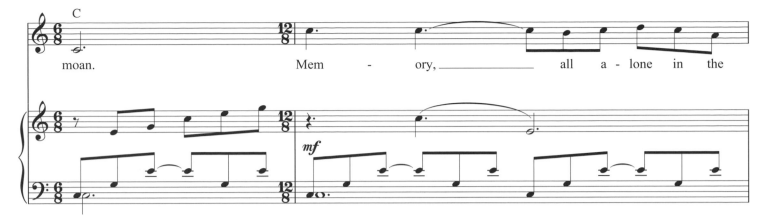

moan. Mem - ory, _____ all a - lone in the

moon - light. _____ I can smile at the old days, _____ I was beau - ti - ful

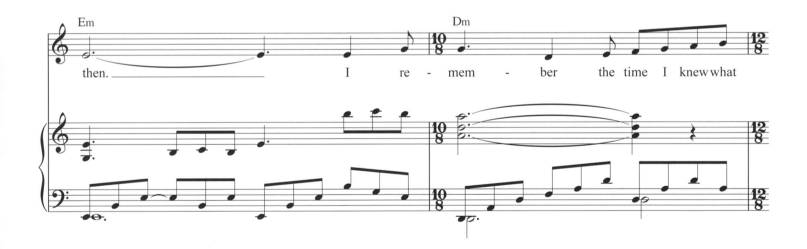

then. _____ I re - mem - ber the time I knew what

hap-pi-ness was. _____ Let the mem - ory live a - gain.

Ev - 'ry street lamp seems to beat _____ a

fa - tal - is - tic warn - ing.

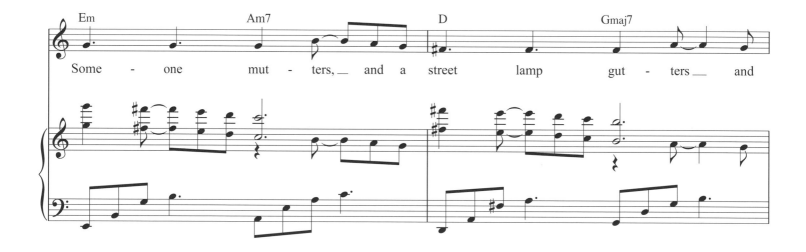

Some - one mut - ters, _ and a street lamp gut - ters _ and

soon it will be morn - ing.

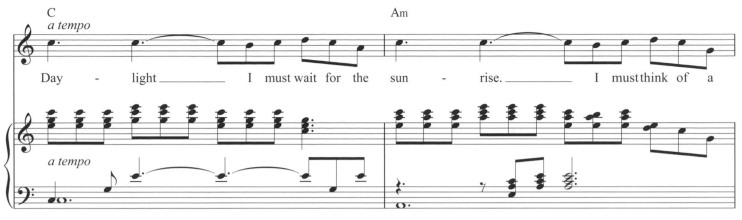

Day - light _____ I must wait for the sun - rise. _____ I must think of a

new life, _____ and I must-n't give in. _____ When the dawn comes to-night will be a

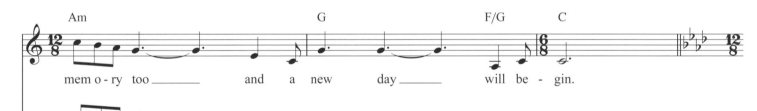

mem o - ry too _____ and a new day _____ will be - gin.

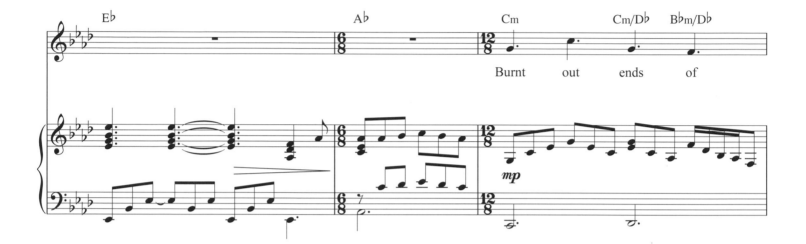

Burnt out ends of

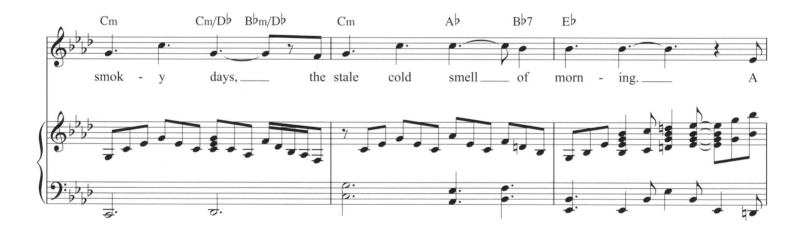

smok-y days,_____ the stale cold smell_____ of morn-ing._____ A

street lamp dies, an-oth-er night is o-ver._ An-oth-er day is

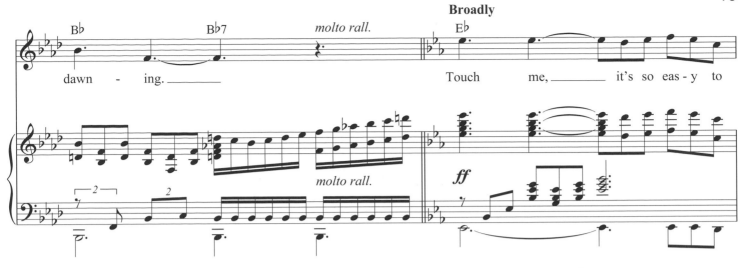

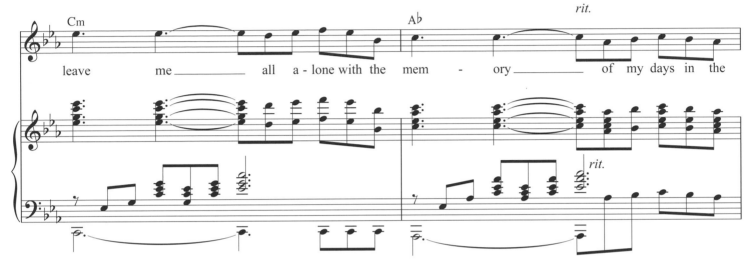

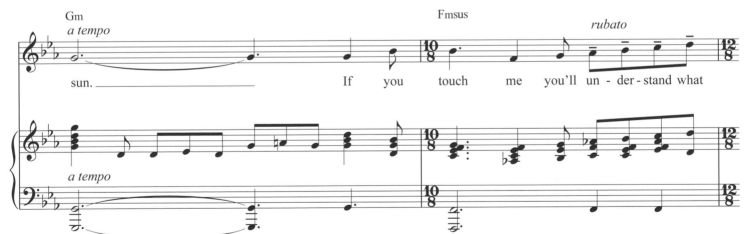

This page has been left blank to facilitate page turns.

MEMORY
from *Cats*
excerpt

Music by ANDREW LLOYD WEBBER
Text by TREVOR NUNN after T.S. ELIOT

THE MUSIC OF THE NIGHT
from *The Phantom of the Opera*

Music by ANDREW LLOYD WEBBER
Lyrics by CHARLES HART
Additional Lyrics by RICHARD STILGOE

Slow - ly, gent - ly, night un - furls its splen - dour; grasp it, sense it, trem - u - lous and ten - der. Turn your face a - way from the gar - ish light of day, turn your thoughts a - way from cold, un - feel - ing light and lis - ten to the mu - sic of the night. Close your eyes and sur - ren - der to your dark - est dreams! Purge your

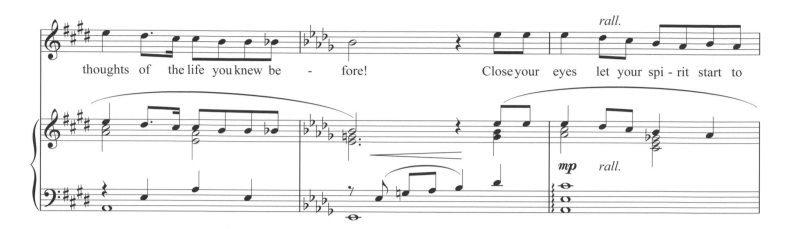

thoughts of the life you knew be - fore! Close your eyes let your spi - rit start to

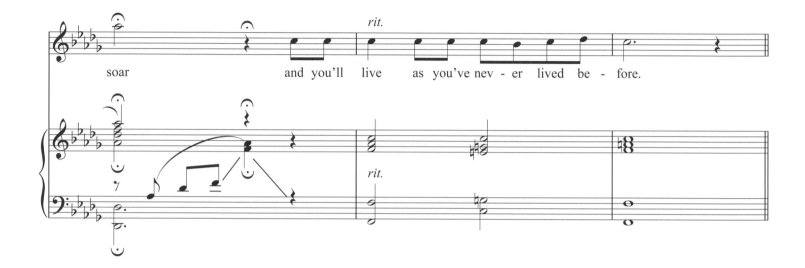

soar and you'll live as you've nev - er lived be - fore.

Soft - ly, deft - ly, mu - sic shall ca - ress you. Hear it, feel it,

se - cret - ly pos - sess you. O - pen up your mind, let your fan - ta - sies un - wind in this

dark-ness which you know you can-not fight, the dark-ness of the mu - sic of the

night. Let your mind start a jour-ney through a strange, new world; leave all

thoughts of the world you knew be - fore. Let your soul take you where you long to

be! On - ly then can you be - long to me.

Float - ing, fall - ing, sweet in - tox - i - ca - tion. Touch me, trust me,

sa - vour each sen - sa - tion. Let the dream be - gin, let your dark - er side give in to the

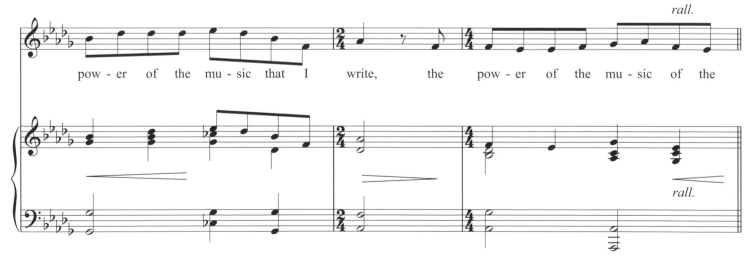

pow - er of the mu - sic that I write, the pow - er of the mu - sic of the

You a-lone can make my song take flight, help me make the mu-sic of the

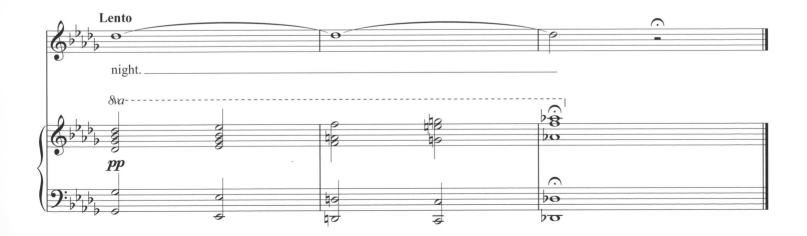

night.

THE MUSIC OF THE NIGHT
from *The Phantom of the Opera*
excerpt

Music by ANDREW LLOYD WEBBER
Lyrics by CHARLES HART
Additional Lyrics by RICHARD STILGOE

mind start a jour-ney through a strange, new world; leave all

thoughts of the world you knew be - fore. Let your soul take you where you long to

be! On - ly then can you be-long to me.

SEEING IS BELIEVING
from *Aspects of Love*

Music by ANDREW LLOYD WEBBER
Lyrics by DON BLACK and CHARLES HART

Andante con moto

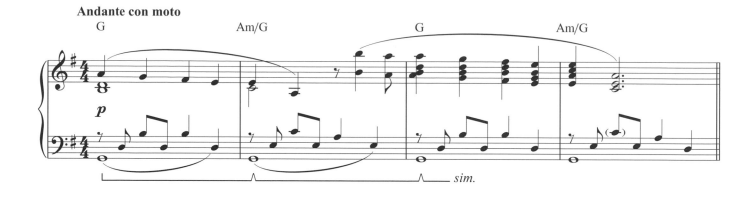

ALEX:

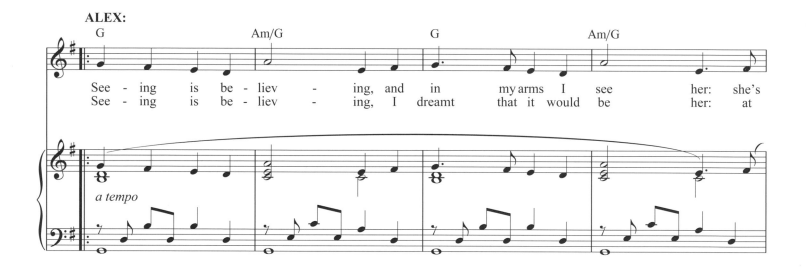

See - ing is be - liev - ing, and in my arms I see her: she's
See - ing is be - liev - ing, I dreamt that it would be her: at

here, real - ly here, real - ly mine now.
last life is full, life is fine now.

This song for Alex and Rose has been adapted as a solo for this edition.

She seems at home here... Whatever happens, one thing is certain:

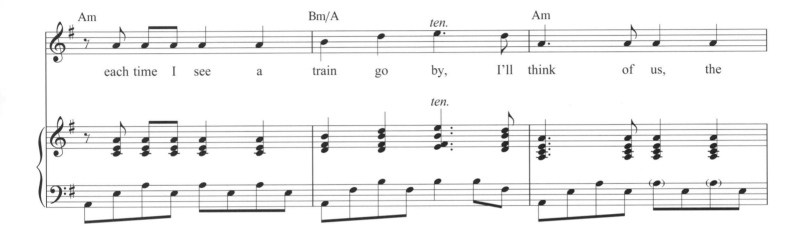

each time I see a train go by, I'll think of us, the

night, the sky forever.

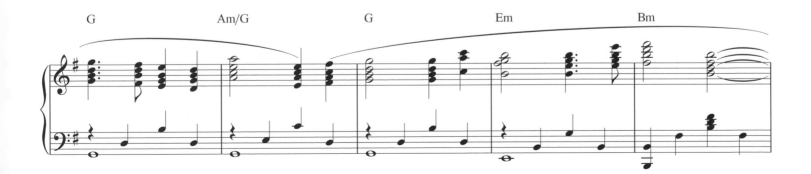

She's warm and she's wild and ap-peal - ing. I feel I know her...

rubato

See - ing is be - liev - ing, and I like ____ what I see here. I

a tempo

like where I am, what I'm feel - ing. What are we do - ing?

Can you be-lieve it? A starv-ing ac-tress and a star-struck boy. Who

knows? Who cares? Let's just en-joy the mo - ment.

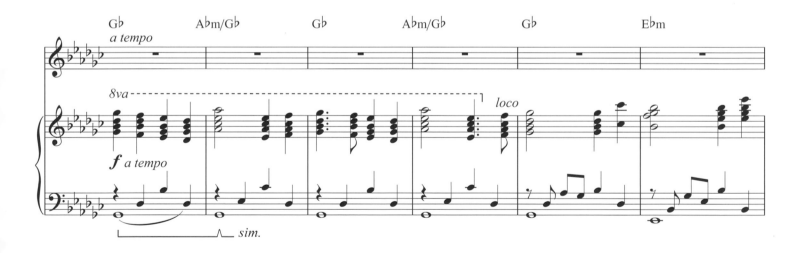

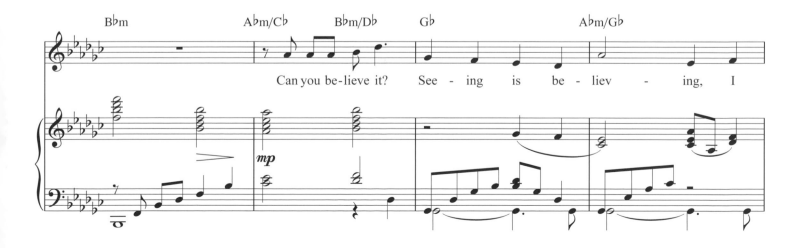

Can you be-lieve it? See - ing is be - liev - ing, I

nev - er thought I'd be here. Is this real - ly me, am I

dream - ing? No way of know-ing where this is lead-ing,

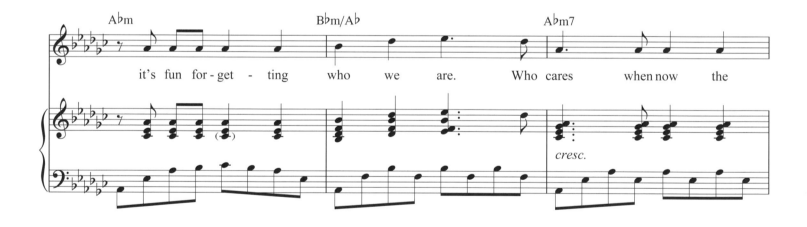

it's fun for - get - ting who we are. Who cares when now the

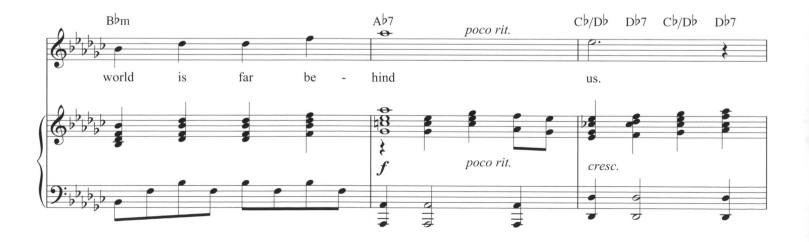

world is far be - hind us.

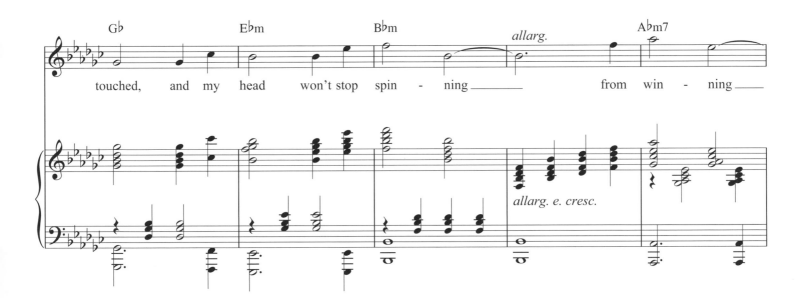

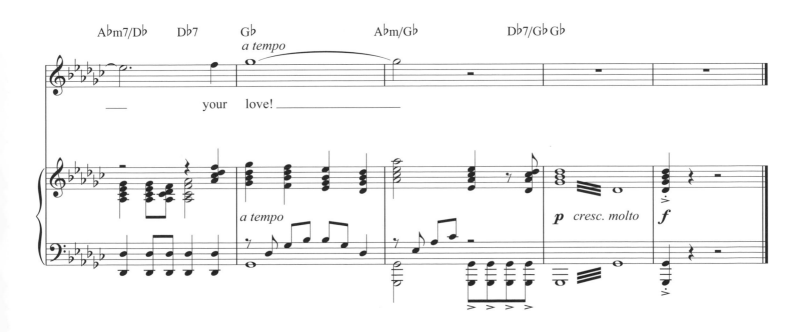

SEEING IS BELIEVING
from *Aspects of Love*
excerpt

Music by ANDREW LLOYD WEBBER
Lyrics by DON BLACK and CHARLES HART

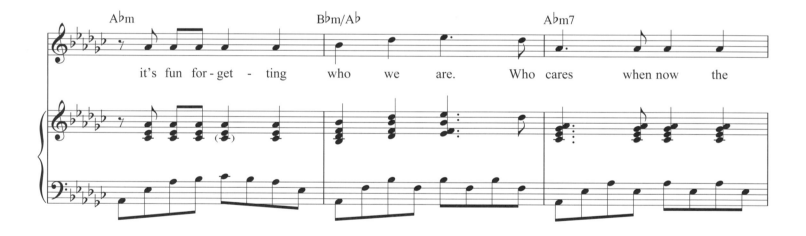

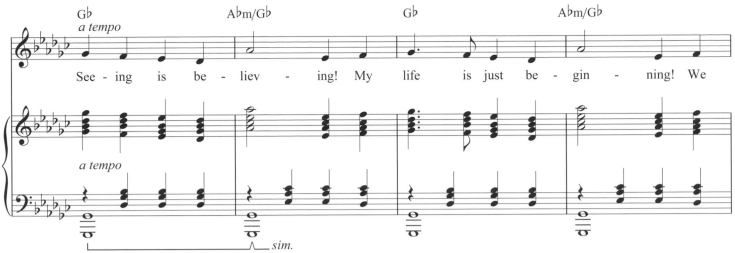

See - ing is be - liev - ing! My life is just be - gin - ning! We

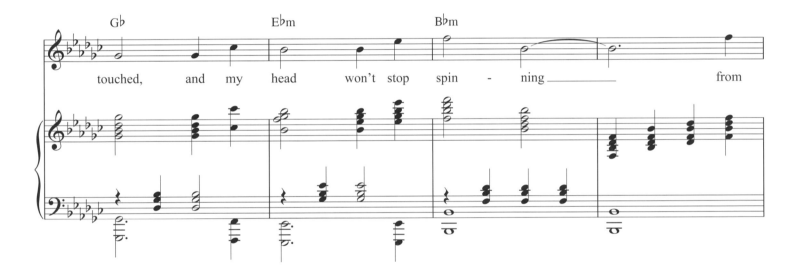

touched, and my head won't stop spin - ning _____ from

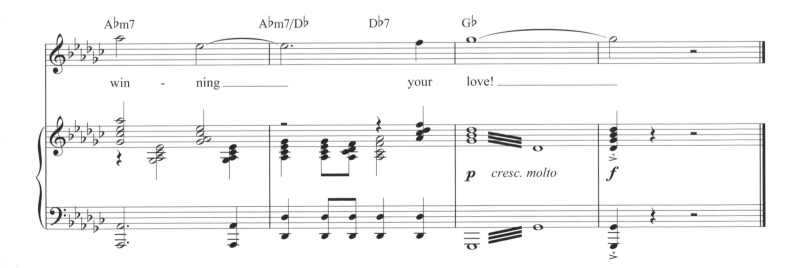

win - ning _____ your love! _____

This page has been left blank to facilitate page turns.

WHEN I CLIMB TO THE TOP OF MOUNT ROCK

from *School of Rock*

Music by ANDREW LLOYD WEBBER
Lyrics by GLENN SLATER

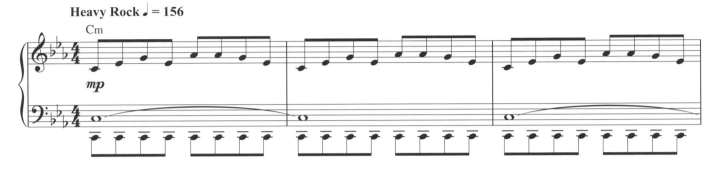

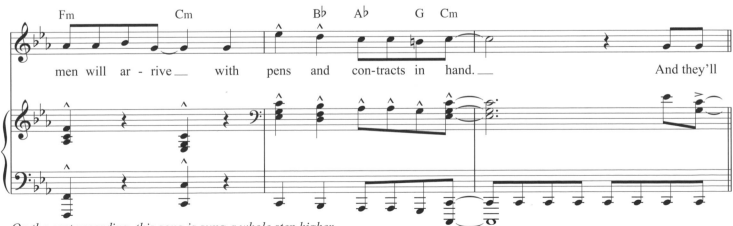

On the cast recording, this song is sung a whole step higher.

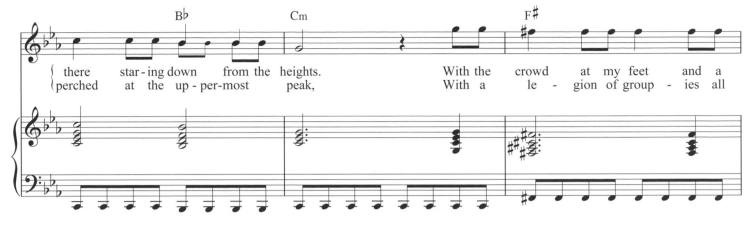

there star-ing down from the heights. / perched at the up-per-most peak,
With the crowd at my feet and a

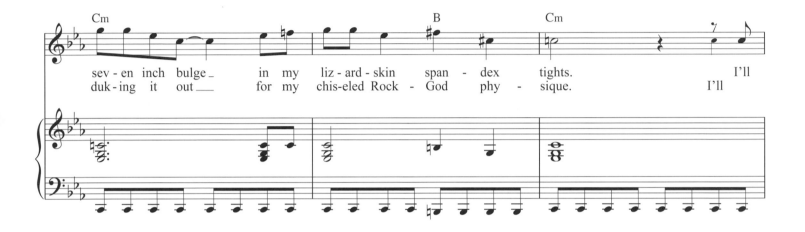

sev-en inch bulge in my liz-ard-skin span-dex tights. / duk-ing it out for my chis-eled Rock - God phy - sique.
I'll

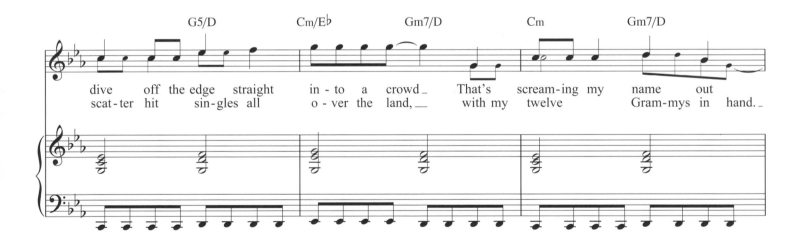

dive off the edge straight in-to a crowd That's scream-ing my name out / scat-ter hit sin-gles all o-ver the land, with my twelve Gram-mys in hand.

To Coda

loud And the gates will un - lock / And the fan - boys will flock

at the top of Mount Rock! I'll be

blow-ing out amps playing Sta-di-um shows On my sold-out ga-lac-tic tour

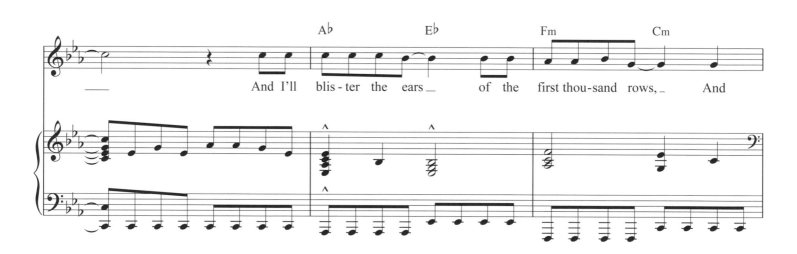

And I'll blis-ter the ears of the first thou-sand rows, And

leave while they beg for more. Then I'll pop the cham-pagne and the

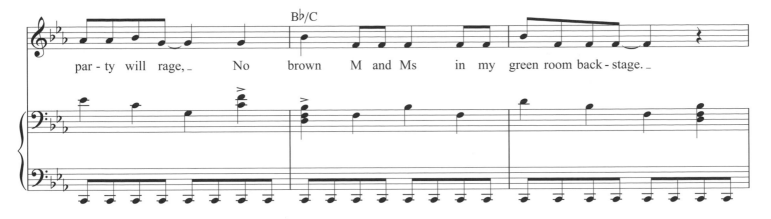

par - ty will rage, _ No brown M and Ms in my green room back - stage. _

Big - ger than Hen - drix and Clap - ton and Page, and the rest...

End of Half time feel

the all - time best...!

When I

D.S. al Coda

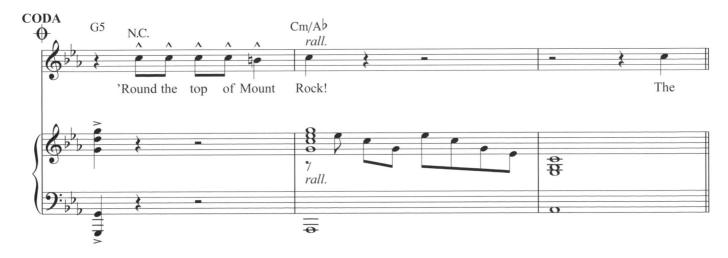

CODA

'Round the top of Mount Rock!

The

Slightly slower

Bb/D   Ab/Eb   Cm/G   Cm   Bb

doub-ters and the hat-ers and the hip-sters let 'em laugh. Soon they'll all be beg-gin' for my

Ab   Cm   G7/D   Dm7b5   Ab

road-ie's au-to-graph. I know my time is com-in'. Well, hope-ful-ly it's com-in'. I'm

Dbmaj7/Ab   G   Ebsus/Db   G

pret-ty sure it's com-in' an-y day Once they hear me play... ___

Tempo I

Cm

Then the dreams that I've had ___ since the day I turned ten ___ Will be

mp

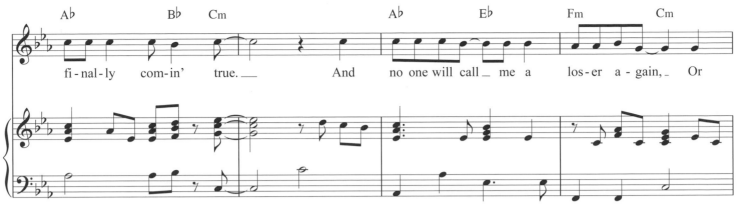

fi - nal - ly com - in' true. ___ And no one will call ___ me a los - er a - gain, ___ Or

tell me what I can't do ___ So I'll hold my head high and keep

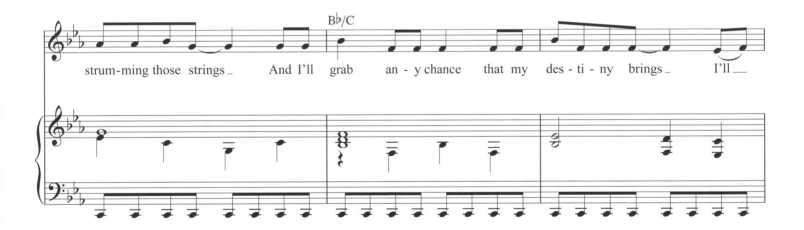

strum - ming those strings ___ And I'll grab an - y chance that my des - ti - ny brings ___ I'll ___

rise and I'll rise and I'll rise on the wings of my song

up where I be - long.   And I'll

climb to the top of Mount Rock   and be part of that heav-en-ly scene   With

O - din and Zeus   on the bass and the drums   And__ Thor play-ing tam - bou -

rine   And El - vis and Jan - is and Kurt will ap - pear   And

Je - sus will toss me a beer. And we'll jam 'round the

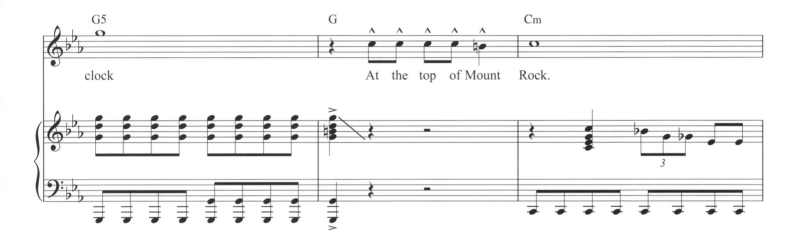

clock At the top of Mount Rock.

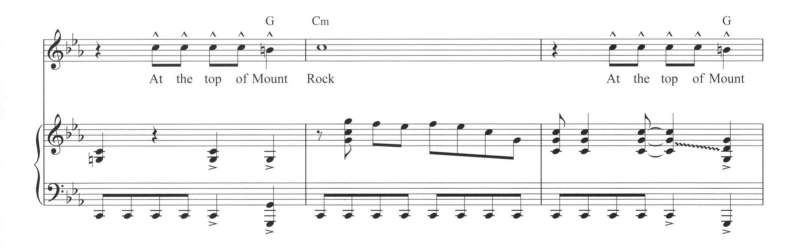

At the top of Mount Rock At the top of Mount

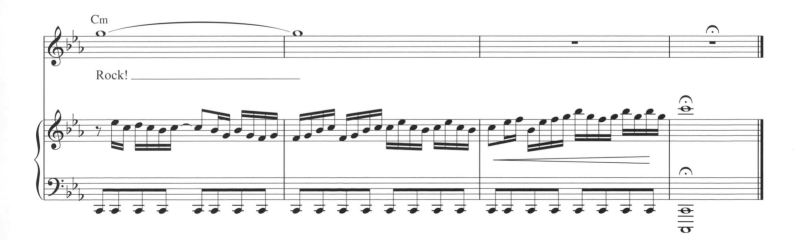

Rock! _____

WHEN I CLIMB TO THE TOP OF MOUNT ROCK

from *School of Rock*

excerpt

Music by ANDREW LLOYD WEBBER
Lyrics by GLENN SLATER

And I'll climb to the top of Mount Rock and be part of that heav-en-ly scene With

O-din and Zeus on the bass and the drums And Thor play-ing tam-bou-

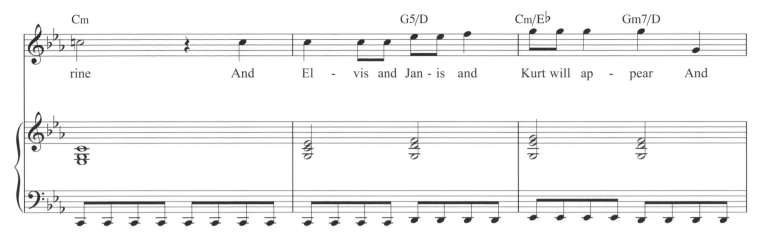

rine   And   El - vis and Jan - is and   Kurt will ap - pear   And

Je - sus will   toss me   a   beer.   And   we'll   jam   'round   the

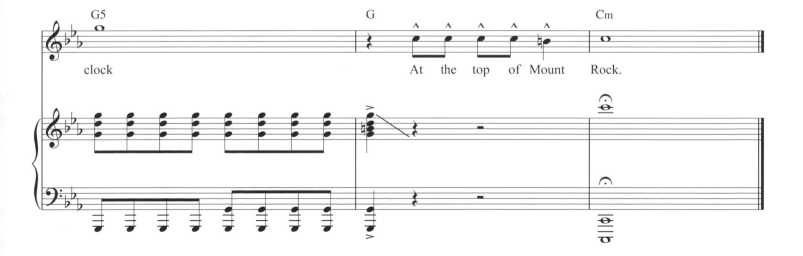

clock   At   the   top   of Mount   Rock.